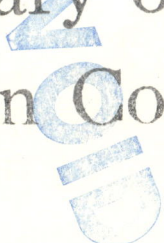

ENGLISH MUSIC

ENGLISH MUSIC

by

SIR WILLIAM H. HADOW

WITH AN INTRODUCTION
BY R. VAUGHAN WILLIAMS.

BOOKS FOR LIBRARIES PRESS
FREEPORT, NEW YORK

First Published 1931
Reprinted 1972

780.942
H131e

INTERNATIONAL STANDARD BOOK NUMBER:
0-8369-6773-9

LIBRARY OF CONGRESS CATALOG CARD NUMBER:
74-38356

PRINTED IN THE UNITED STATES OF AMERICA
BY
NEW WORLD BOOK MANUFACTURING CO., INC.
HALLANDALE, FLORIDA 33009

80-422

INTRODUCTION

CAN we claim music as part of our national heritage? Are we not the "land without music"? Did not Charles Lamb refuse to music the title of a liberal art? Do not our friends abroad and our enemies at home insist that music is outside our sphere? Only the other day a writer in one of our important London papers, in lamenting the end of the German Opera season and the reign of the cheaper form of Italian Opera, said that all the musicians among the audience had departed and that only the British remained. It is curious, by the way, that the "British" who watched these operas from the stalls all had guttural voices, while the "British" from the gallery shouted "bravo" and "brava" with a very correct accent, and smelt strongly of Soho. Nevertheless they were obviously deaf to the higher implications of music, therefore they must be "British." It is the old story, our own country can do nothing right. It was so in the eighteenth century. Professor Trevelyan in his *Blenheim* writes: "Nothing is more striking than the inability of the English to stand by their native traditions in art." Have we any native traditions? for surely without them our art is meaningless. If our music is of any value it must strike roots down into its native soil. Miss Margaret Kennedy entirely misunderstands the mind of the musician in the scene which she imagines between Sanger and the workman. Any musician who is worth his salt realizes that his ultimate sanction rests with the *en masse*. Possibly Miss Kennedy was misled by the analogy of painters, for painters, at all events in Chelsea, inherit from Whistler a snobbery which has not yet disappeared.

If we are the "land without music" then this lack of music must go down to the very foundations of our life. But is this so? Do not recent discoveries show at the basis of our musical life a power of musical invention and a poetical impulse unsurpassed anywhere? Can the primitive music of any nation show anything to compare with the grim fantasy of "The trees they do grow high," or the delicate beauty of "Searching for lambs." But here our snobbery comes into play again. That an English countryman can invent beautiful tunes must be nonsense. Those delightful Austrian peasants perhaps, or those wild wicked Russians, or those dear picturesque Italian contadini; even the Hebrides are just within the pale, but "Hodge"! I use this name advisedly because it has been actually used in a sneering reference to our English folk-songs, not at a suburban debating society of the "'eighties," but by the accredited musical critic of a cultivated journal of the present day.

Nevertheless, our foreign critics sometimes understand us better than we do ourselves—and the one artistic activity which foreign students and teachers come to England to learn from us is the study of our own national folk-songs and dances.

Now let us look at the matter from another point

of view. Are these occasional displays of brilliance which mark the musical history of England mere accidents? These accidents, these freaks, do not occur except in the minds of sentimental novelists. The genius who springs from nowhere and does something that no one has thought of before is contrary to the facts of artistic history. The great man closes a period, he does not inaugurate it. It is the small men, the Monteverdes, the Emmanuel Bachs, the Liszts and the Stravinskis who are the innovators, forerunners who prepare the way for those who are to sum up the work of a musical generation. And so our great men, Byrd, Purcell, Sullivan, Parry, Elgar, could not have existed without the crowd of small fry who preceded them.

English music is like the tree which flowers once in a hundred years; but unless the tree were alive there would be no flower and its life depends, not only on its intrinsic vitality but on the soil on which it grows, the rain that falls on it and the sun which shines on it, the care with which the soil is dug and turned and weeds are got rid of and pestiferous insects warded off. The plant of English musical culture is a small and tender growth, for the very reason that those whose business it was to nurture it have failed to do so. Instead they have done their best to stifle it, not necessarily from malice but because they did not realize its existence. They were looking for flaunting hydrangeas and exotic mimosa and finding none they declared there were no flowers to be seen, having failed to notice the modest violets and daisies that were hidden in the grass.

If we want to find the groundwork of our English culture we must look below the surface—not to the grand events chronicled in the newspapers but to the unobtrusive quartet parties which meet week after week to play or sing in their own houses, to the village choral societies whose members trudge miles through rain and snow to work steadily for a concert or competition in some ghastly parish room with a cracked piano and a smelly oil lamp where one week there is no tenor because at the best there are only two, and one has a cold and the other being the village doctor is always called out at the critical moment; and there they sit setting their teeth so as to wrench the heart out of this mysterious piece of music which they are starting to learn for the coming competition.

"Competition," you will say, "that is just the sporting spirit, nothing to do with art." Well, unless we have learnt that art comes to the Englishman unconsciously we have yet to learn the first thing about that spirit which has produced our great poetry, our great drama and our great pictures.

The average Englishman does not care to parade his bravery, his patriotism, his artistic ideals or his spiritual longings—but they are there all the same. Professor Dent told me that he was much shocked because while the young composers in Germany and Italy were never tired of talking about art, their contemporaries in England preferred to discuss football matches. Quite so, in England we don't talk about these things, we just do them.

It is said that England has never produced a virtuoso. Of executants this is possibly true, though surely Elgar and Holst are virtuosi among composers.

The virtuoso performer is the foaming crest of the wave, very delightful to look at, but the real power of the wave lies below the surface. We can get on very well without the virtuoso executant; he always has a touch of the showman about him and the English are not good showmen. We want to do honest work without fuss and, if necessary, without recognition, and if we would be true to ourselves we must produce music which will represent that side of our national character. Why ask for more? If we cannot produce diamonds let us not waste our time manufacturing paste.

It is in such surroundings as these and such only that our Byrds, our Purcells, our Sullivans, our Parrys and our Elgars will find their congenial soil. We are so afraid of being parochial. The truth is we are nothing like parochial enough. We are always judging ourselves by foreign standards and wondering what foreigners will think of us. What does it matter? Is art to be standardized as if it were an electric fitting or a safety razor? What will it profit the Englishman if he tries to pose as a Parisian or a Berliner? Will he not be the laughing-stock both of the country which he has deserted and of that whose outward characteristics he vainly tries to adopt? Cosmopolitanism in art means loss of vitality. It is the stream pressing against its narrow banks which will turn the mill wheel. In every nation except ours the power of nationalism in art is recognized. It is this very advocacy of a colourless cosmopolitanism which makes one occasionally despair of England as a musical nation. A few years ago someone invented the very foolish phrase, "A good European." The best European is the most convinced Nationalist, not the Chauvinist but he who believes that all countries should be different and friendly rather than all alike and at enmity. I cannot sum this up better than by quoting the noble words of Stresemann in 1926: "The man who serves humanity best is he who, rooted in his own nation, develops his spiritual and moral endowments to their highest capacity, so that growing beyond the limits of his own nation, he is able to give something to the whole of humanity, as the great ones of all nations have done."

Our English heritage of music goes quietly on, ignored, stamped on, untended and uncared for; a very Cinderella of the family of arts, but unobtrusively pursuing its way; occasionally when the moment is ripe showing a timid flower, none the less lovely for being unnoticed by those whose eyes are everywhere but on the ground at their feet. Did not our language go through the same phase? Let me again quote Professor Trevelyan, who, for a self-styled Philistine, has an extraordinary quantity of pregnant things to say about the arts: "There is no more romantic episode in the history of man than this underground growth and unconscious self-preparation of a despised island *patois*, destined ere long to burst forth into sudden blaze, to be spoken in every quarter of the globe, and to produce a literature with which only that of ancient Hellas is comparable."

Music is the youngest of the arts, just as I suppose

poetry is the oldest. Will a future historian be able to use words like these of our music? It is not impossible. The great composer of the twentieth century is yet to come. By all the historic precedents he should be born in 1985 just as John Sebastian Bach was born in 1685, and he will be born in that country which is the best prepared for him. The artistic surroundings into which Bach was born were distinctly "parochial." His predecessors knew nothing of "world movements" in art, but worked quietly and conscientiously as local organists and music directors to provide the artistic expression of the simple-minded people among whom they lived. Thus quietly and unostentatiously they built up the great tradition which made possible the advent of the greatest musician of all times.

Is there not a moral for us English here?

R. VAUGHAN WILLIAMS.

PREFACE

THIS is an attempt to trace the course of music in England from the earliest records to those of the present day. Chapter I deals with the origins of our composition both sacred and secular; with the encouragement of Church music by St. Dunstan and its censure by Aelred of Rievaulx, both in their way significant; with the early knowledge and use of instruments; with the Winchester Troper and the Worcester volume of mediæval harmony; with the scholars and theorists of the time; with the Reading Rota and the Agincourt song; and reaches its culmination in the work of John Dunstable. The next two chapters are occupied with the Tudor period; with the Old Hall and Eton manuscripts, with questions of Royal patronage and Ecclesiastical controversy; with the work of Robert Carver; with the three groups of Tudor composers, from Fayrfax to Aston, from Taverner to Farrant, and so to Tallis and Byrd and the madrigalists and song-writers. Chapter IV starts at the point of transition with Orlando Gibbons, and follows the course of events through the Commonwealth and the Restoration, treating of masque and opera and the growth of popular melody, and so ascending to the famous school of the Chapel Royal—Pelham Humfrey, Blow, and Henry Purcell. After Purcell's death came the dark age, described in Chapter V, when our native composition, a feeble luminary at the best, was dimmed by the splendour of Handel and further obscured by the prevalence of Italian opera. Our chief representative was Arne, after him Croft and Greene and Boyce, and although we popularized " God Save the King " we seem to have derived its melody from an earlier age. Chapter VI traces the origin and growth of our English Renascence first through Field and Sterndale Bennett and S. S. Wesley, then with Arthur Sullivan and his contemporaries in opera, then with the full maturity of Parry and Stanford and Sir Edward Elgar. The last chapter summarizes the leaders of the present generation from Vaughan Williams and Holst to Bax and Walton, deals with the development of folk music, the discovery of the Tudor classics, and the influence on both of new musical idioms and resources, indicating the advance which we have already made and the auguries which it gives of a more extensive progress in the future.

Much of my information has naturally been gained from Grove, from the Oxford History, and from the critical writers of the eighteenth and early nineteenth centuries. Beside these I am specially indebted to Cobbett's Encyclopædia, to Davey's *History of English Music*, and to Dr. Ernest Walker's invaluable *History of Music in England*. To these and to many other helpers I would offer full and grateful acknowledgment.

CONTENTS

ENGLISH MUSIC

CHAPTER I

THE BEGINNINGS

" A POVERTY-STRICKEN country: you will not find one scruple of silver in the entire island. Your only hope of booty is from slaves— and I can hardly suppose that you would expect a Briton to have any knowledge of music or letters."[1] That, in brief, is Cicero's opinion of our countrymen. It is not perhaps entirely unbiassed: if Pompey instead of Cæsar had been leading the expedition we might have received a more favourable judgment. But the fact remains that our first introduction to the civilized world is in terms of unmitigated contempt, and it is little consolation to reflect that the beginnings of Roman culture would have fared almost as ill at the hands of the Greeks, or of Greek culture at the hands of the Egyptians.

We need not dwell here on the part played by the Druids in our early civilization. Strabo[2] ascribes to them an elaborate ritual of sacrifice, some empirical knowledge of science, and the practice of magic which seems to have included the use of ceremonial chants; but the evidence is too fragmentary and uncertain to be of much avail. We are on more

---

[1] Cicero, *ad Atticum*, IV, 16.   [2] IV, 275.

solid ground when we come to the record of
Agricola's occupation, which took place in the latter
part of the first century, A.D. After subduing the
country he gave it every encouragement in the arts
of peace. He instituted schools in which the young
princes were taught the humanities, and he stimu-
lated them to the highest efforts by tactfully extolling
their quickness of apprehension as compared with
the plodding industry of the Gauls.[1] It is germane
to note that his secretary at the time was the learned
grammarian, Demetrius of Tarsus, who taught
Greek and Latin at York and who was specially
interested in religion and religious music.[2] We have
already travelled some distance from the unlettered
barbarians of Cicero.

When, therefore, the Christian missionaries began
their work in Britain they found awaiting them a
long if slender tradition of humanity and learning.
There can be no doubt that in this matter Ireland
and Wales were ahead of England; though St.
Patrick is said to have come from "the lower waters
of the Severn," and St. David to have been educated
at York. But a few years before St. David's death
came St. Augustine to Canterbury, and there
opened a new chapter not only in our religious
history, but in that of our general culture and
education.

His main work as an administrator falls outside
our present scope: among its fruits was the institution in Kent of a school of Church Music which long
held throughout England a position of undisputed
supremacy. And in the next generation came Wilfrid

---

[1] Tacitus, *Agricola*, ch. 21.   [2] Demetrius, *On Style*, ch. 71.

and Theodore of Tarsus, the latter of whom was the first Archbishop of Canterbury whose rule was accepted by the entire English Church, and who made visitations up and down the country giving instruction "in Holy Writ, poetry, astronomy, and arithmetic." One result of the new teaching is noted by Bede,[1] and concerns us here:

> "From that time also they began in all the churches of the English to learn sacred music which till then had been known only in Kent. And the first singing-master in the Churches of the Northumbrians was Eddi, surnamed Stephen, invited from Kent by the most reverend Wilfrid, who was the first bishop of the English nation that taught the Churches of the English the Catholic mode of life."

A significant story is told about Aldhelm, disciple of Theodore, who was Abbot of Malmesbury and afterwards Bishop of Sherborne, one of the most notable figures in the literature of the seventh century. It is said that in order to attract a congregation he used to take his harp to the market-cross at Malmesbury and there sing ditties beloved of the people until they gathered round him, when he gradually substituted the hymns and canticles which he wished them to learn. Be that as it may, he was undoubtedly a great song-writer, and he may well have turned to ends of edification that natural love of music which the Church has always found to be one of the most powerful of her allies.

[1] *Eccl. Hist.*, iv, 2.

During all this period there spread in ever-widening circles the practice of secular song. In Wales and Ireland the bards formed a separate and honourable class: to their ranks only free men were admitted; they held by law the right of unquestioned hospitality; they stood next in rank to the priest and the warrior. In England, especially after the Nordic invasions, they fell into two classes, the dividing line of which was not always clearly observed. The higher and more distinguished artist was the Scop, who was usually attached to a court and was often of noble blood: the lower and more popular was the Gleeman, a professional entertainer who sang his songs and performed his feats of skill during the circuit of the ale-horn, and who was liberally rewarded for his services by the company at large. It was not long before their influence permeated society from end to end. As Mr. Waller says in the *Cambridge History of English Literature*[1]:

"The gift of song was by no means confined to professionals. Often the chieftain himself took up the harp and sang, perhaps a little boastfully, of great deeds.[2] At the other end of the scale we hear of the man whose duty it was to take a turn at the stable-work of a monastery being sad at heart when the harp was passed round and he had no music to give[3]; and the plough lad when he had drawn his first furrow revealed both his

[1] Vol. i, p. 3.
[2] So Hrothgar in *Beowulf*. Alfred the Great was a famous minstrel.
[3] Cædmon: see Bede, iv, 24.

capacity for song and his nature worship, with faint if any traces of Christianity, in lines perhaps among the oldest our language has to show:

'Hale be thou earth, mother of men!
Fruitful be thou in the arms of the God:
Be filled with thy fruit for the fare-need of man.'"

It is worth adding that much of our earliest lyric poetry seems to have been composed by minstrels, not by men of letters. We are definitely told this in the poems of *Widsith* and *Deor*, and there is evidence that the rule may apply to others as well. No doubt the melodies were rude and artless, mere forms of recitation, often improvised and more often speedily forgotten, yet they kept alive the joy of musical sound, and served as the vehicle of a more enduring art. So the threads gather together—the love of music which seems inherent in our whole people, the discipline and order of Roman civilization, the poetry of Celt and Dane and Saxon, the growth of material prosperity with its enhanced opportunities of patronage and encouragement, and strongest of all formative influences, a religion which was inspiring the nation's life with its own spiritual message and which was wise enough to press into service every worthy form of human activity and aspiration. Through the days of the Heptarchy the seed of music continued to grow in secret, or with but slight and incidental manifestations; then it blossomed and bore fruit in the life and work of St. Dunstan.

His name has been surrounded with an over-

growth of legend so abundant that it is not surprising if his actual achievement has been somewhat
obscured. But the legends themselves are innocent
or grotesque, and when they are cleared away there
remains the monument of a genius who was not
only a great administrator but a great artist as well.[1]

He was born in 924 near Glastonbury, and educated at the Abbey School where, from the earliest
days, he was conspicuous both for the brilliance of
his ability and for the fervour of his devotion. At
the age of twenty-four he was appointed Abbot, and
soon made his monastery widely famous as a centre
of learning and of the arts. In all these pursuits alike
he took the leading part; he was equally celebrated
as painter, calligraphist, and craftsman in gold and
silver, a scholar of profound erudition and a master
of all the sciences known in his day. But the study
nearest to his heart was music, and especially (which
is noticeable) the music of instruments: "sicut
David," as Capgrave says, "psalterium sumens,
citharam percutiens, modificans organa, cimbala
tangens." There is a characteristic story that once
when he was sitting at his table "desyning a stole,"
his harp, which was hanging on the wall, sounded
of itself, and inspired him with one of his most
famous compositions. Like many men of high-
strung temperament he was subject to visions which
came to him sometimes in the night, sometimes at

[1] The chief authorities for his life are (1) an anonymous contemporary who is known as Auctor B.; (2) Osbern who was his
junior but overlapped with him; (3) Capgrave who compiled a
biography in the fourteenth century. There is also a brief account
of him in *The Golden Legend*.

the serving of the Mass; and almost all those which are recorded attain their climax in an outburst of music, which, we are told, he was able afterwards to remember and dictate. The names of a few among them are recorded: "O Rex gentium dominator omnium," "Gaudent in cœlis animæ sanctorum," and above all his reputed masterpiece the "Kyrie Rex splendens," which was long employed in the Sarum use on his festival and on that of St. Michael. The full text of this noble hymn is accessible in Capgrave's biography and cries aloud for music to replace the lost melodies of its original composer.

With his public career as chief adviser to the throne, as Bishop of Worcester, and of London, and as Archbishop of Canterbury we are not here concerned. It is probable that the stress and labour of tireless administration left him scant leisure for the pursuit of the arts (although one of his visions is dated in the reign of Edgar, who appointed him to his successive sees), in any case he bears the name of the greatest English musician before the Conquest, and although none of his writing has survived the vicissitudes of time we may still hold in reverence one who as a statesman was the precursor of Becket and Wolsey and as an artist of Dunstable and Taverner and William Byrd.

It has been said that his chief predilection was for the music of instruments; and this statement requires a word of elucidation and comment. We have no evidence that there was any kind of independent and self-contained instrumental music in the time of Dunstan: indeed the evidence is strong to the contrary. The only two outlets for musical

expression were song and dance, of which the latter
was developed from a primitive instinct for the
delight and excitement of gesture, and was still held
in great disfavour by serious musicians. Cicero
expresses the Roman view when he tells us that "no
man ever dances when he is sober" (Aristotle says
the same about amateur singing), and the war
dances and sword dances of the northern tribes were
evidently gymnastic displays which needed no more
accompaniment than was sufficient to mark the
rhythm.[1] To this may be added as further testimony
that the only system of musical notation as yet
known was a scheme of conventional signs, called
neumes, which were written above the syllables of
the text and marked, without any indication of pitch
or measure, the bare rise and fall of the singing voice.
The discovery of staff-notation is certainly not earlier
than the eleventh century,[2] and the method out of
which it was developed can have been used only for
vocal music. That there were instrumental accompaniments of some kind is abundantly clear: but
they must have been confined either to doubling the
voice part or to supplying it with improvisations
which depended on the skill and fancy of the performer. Such was, undoubtedly, the instrumental
music of Dunstan, and it is noticeable that all the
compositions attributed to him bear the names of
the sacred texts to which they were set.

Many of the instruments current in England about
this time are depicted in an illumination of which the

[1] See for instance Tacitus, *Germania*, ch. 24.
[2] See Miss Sylvia Warner's account of it: *Oxford History of
Music*, Introductory Volume, ch. 4.

original is in the University Library at Glasgow and
a reproduction in Grove's Dictionary.[1] The date of
the MS. is 1175, which is later than our actual
period, but the growth of musical invention in
these early days was so slow that the collection may
be taken as fairly typical. In the middle of the picture
David ("sicut Dunstan") is playing a harp: above
him in a gallery two athletic youths are running to
and fro beating with mallets a series of chime-bells,
all apparently of the same size, so that they are not
intended to be melodic; at his feet are four musicians
playing respectively on rebec, pan-pipe, recorder,
and viol: three more in medallions at the foot, are
playing on psaltery, handbells, and organistrum.[2]
There are some curious omissions—the trumpet,
much beloved by mediæval Italian painters; the
drum, which set the rhythm for pageant and ceremonial; the pipe and tabor, which brought delight to
rustic merry making; and, above all, the organ, which
though still clumsy in construction and limited in
range was beginning to assume its pride of place
and had been known in England since the time of
Aldhelm. Its absence is the more conspicuous
because it was specially associated with St. Dunstan,
who not only was a famous player but built organs
for the abbeys of Malmesbury and Abingdon and

[1] Grove, Third Edition, vol. iv, p. 334.
[2] The rebec and the viol were two kinds of bowed instruments,
the former held to the shoulder, the latter supported on the knees.
The recorder was a fipple flute, of the same ancestry as the flageolet.
The psaltery was a prototype of the harpsichord, a frame of strings
which were plucked with the finger or a plectrum. The organistrum
was a hurdy-gurdy, a combination of keyboard and strings
"bowed" with a wheel.

for other churches throughout the country. Still
with all deductions it is a collection of great interest
and makes us the more regret that we know so little
of "what was piped or harped."

The last important musical work which belongs
to the period of the Heptarchy is the compilation of
the so-called Winchester Troper,[1] which is assigned
by most scholars to the early part of the eleventh
century. The MS., which is now in the library of
Corpus Christi College, Cambridge, is very difficult
to decipher as it is written in neumes without any
distinction of pitch, measure, or clef; but at least it
indicates a rude and elementary form of two-part
harmony and even of parts moving in contrary
motion. It is thus of great historical value and when
subject to further investigation may throw a considerable amount of light on early part-writing,
especially that form known as Organum or Dia-
phony, and its relation to the subsequent method of
descant. Such examples as have been conjecturally
deciphered and transcribed are of the most extreme
simplicity; pure and devotional in tone but almost
ascetic in their disdain of charm and craftsmanship.

A vast change was effected by the Norman
Conquest, which brought with it a new sense of

---

[1] The name Trope was given sometimes to the music, sometimes
to the music and words together, of interpolated liturgical texts
which were inserted in the Ordinary of the Mass, either for variety
or to mark some special commemoration. Dunstan's "Kyrie Rex
splendens" was a trope and so were others of the same time. The
volumes in which these tropes were collected bore the name of
Tropers. The practice of interpolating them was discontinued in
the sixteenth century, though one or two examples survive as
separate compositions: *e.g.* " Of the Father's love begotten."

luxury and amenity: which ennobled our architecture, remodelled our language, and taught new melodies to our literature. Its influence on our music was at first not wholly for good: we yielded all too easily to the new enchantments and followed with too ready steps along the paths of pleasure and excitement. By the middle of the twelfth century our Church music had carried elaboration to the point of excess, and had provoked from the saintly Aelred of Rivaulx a severe and unsparing rebuke.[1]

"Whence," he asks, "hath the Church so many organs and musicall instruments? To what purpose, I pray you, is that terrible blowing of belloes, expressing rather the crakes of thunder than the sweetnesse of a voyce? To what purpose serves that contraction and inflection of the voyce? This man sings a base, that a small meane, another a treble, a fourth divides, and cuts asunder, as it were, certaine middle notes: one while the voyce is strained, anon it is remitted, now it is dashed and then againe it is inlarged with a lowder sound. Sometimes, which is a shame to speake, it is enforced into a horse's neighing: sometimes the masculine vigour being laid aside it is sharpened into the shrillnesse of a woman's voyce: now and then it is writhed and retorted with a certaine artificial circumvolution. Sometimes thou may'st see a man with an open mouth, not to sing, but to breathe out his last gaspe by shutting in his breath, and by a certaine

[1] *Speculum Charitatis*, ii. 23. I copy Prynne's translation which is quoted in Henry Davey's *History of English Music*, p. 19.

ridiculous interception of his voyce as it were to threaten silence. . . . In the meantime the common people standing by, trembling and astonished, admire the sound of the organ, the noyse of the cymballs and musicall instruments, the harmony of the pipes and cornets."

One clause of this indictment is specially notable as attacking a ridiculous convention which had just come into vogue. This was the Hocket (the literal meaning of which is hiccough), a device for interspersing the musical phrase with rests, irrespective of the sense, so that the singer was abruptly silenced in the middle of a word and the whole continuity of the passage sacrificed. It is to Aelred's credit that he struck the first blow which helped to bring this folly to an ignominious end. But apart from this the whole passage is full of interesting topics—the variety of instruments employed in the Church service; the habit, already formed, of straining after emotional and even sensational effects; and, above all, the practice of writing in at least three parts, each of which has an individual character of its own. Clearly the English Church music of the twelfth century, with all its errors and shortcomings, had made considerable advances in the matter of polyphonic resource.

This growth of executive skill, to which Aelred bears reluctant witness, extended also to the popular music of the time. Here our chief authority is Giraldus Cambrensis, or Gerald de Barri, a younger contemporary of Aelred, who was Archdeacon of St. David's during the close of the century. He is

one of the most charming of mediæval writers: a
great traveller, a keen observer, an entertaining
companion: indeed his adventurous disposition
seems to have cost him his prospects of ecclesiastical
preferment, for we are told that he was thrice
proposed for the See of St. David's and thrice
rejected by a papal veto. His allusions to music are
few in number, but highly significant. In the
Topographica Hibernica he pays a warm tribute to the
Irish harpers: "incomparably the best of any nation
that I know," though he adds that those of Wales
and Scotland bid fair to rival them. The Irish, he
says, have two instruments in current use—harp
and bagpipes: the Scotch have three—harp, bagpipes,
and crowd[1]: the Welsh also three—harp, crowd, and
tibia, and it is clear from his description that the
harpers at any rate had moved him by something
more than dexterity. In a later work, the *Descriptio
Cambriæ*, occurs the famous passage on Welsh and
Northumbrian singing which, in spite of one obscure
phrase, remains a *locus classicus* of the history of
music. The Northumbrians, he says, make use of "a
kind of symphonious singing" in two parts, by
natural gift without instruction, and adds that even
the children are proficient in this art. But, as might
be expected, his most enthusiastic encomium is
reserved for his own countrymen. The Welsh, he
says, sing their national songs not in unison but in
as many different parts as there are singers, "uniting
these diversities at length in one consonance and

[1] A bowed instrument with four or six strings, earliest known
ancestor of the violin family. The name is common in Elizabethan
drama.

organic melody under the soft sweetness of B flat."[1]
This last phrase has given much trouble to the
commentators, and no satisfactory explanation is
forthcoming. It is perhaps not irreverent to suggest
that the Archdeacon, who had many other subjects
of study, may have used musical technicalities with
the same freedom as some of our most eminent
poets, and that the passage is of the same order as
"blaring out the mode Palestrina," or noting with
surprise that there are no sharps in the key-signature
of E♮ major. At any rate it does not impair the
value of his testimony, and we may claim a tradition
of at least eight hundred years for our proficiency
in harp and pipes and for the skill and variety of our
community singing.

We do not know what popular melodies Giraldus
heard in his travels or what subtlety of contrapuntal
texture he may have found in the Church services.
But we have an uncontrovertible witness as to their
quality in the Reading Rota, "Sumer is i-cumen in,"[2]
which is dated about 1240, some twenty years after
his death. Some unthinking critics, dazzled by the
splendour of this masterpiece, have come to regard
it as an isolated miracle which shines in the surround-
ing darkness by some force of unaccountable magic.
This conclusion violates every canon of historical
probability and runs, as we have seen, counter to
the known facts of the case. No man could have
composed the Rota whose genius had not been
trained by a long tradition of learning, and nurtured

[1] In unam denique sub B mollis dulcedine blanda consonantiam
et organicam convenientia melodiam,
[2] See Illustration A,

in an atmosphere of artistic beauty and delight. One might as well suppose that there were no painters before Angelico or that he accomplished his work in the caverns of the Troglodytes.

The Rota has been so often described, and is so readily accessible at the present day, that a very few words of commentary may here suffice. It is attributed to John of Fornsete, a Reading monk, and was included in a set of manuscripts preserved at that monastery.[1] The music is set to a delightful lyric, recorded in every English anthology: a welcome to Summer, which is as fresh now as on the day that it was written, and which, like the shepherd boy in Sidney, "pipes as if it should never grow old." The melody has all the charm and lilt of a folksong, it threads its way through one of the most intricate of musical forms, it employs its contrapuntal skill with astonishing mastery and with an ease which never checks or falters, and it is animated throughout by the very spirit of the English countryside; it would have befitted equally the courtiers in Arden and the shearers in the *Winter's Tale*. We have no need to boast that the other nations of Europe can show nothing comparable—their record also may be imperfect and the future may bring our refutation.[2] We are more concerned to note that we have here an achievement which raises our country beyond cavil into the first ranks of musical composition, and assigns to us a place of honour which we held,

[1] It is now in the British Museum: Harl. 978.
[2] Adam de la Halle of Arras (*d. c.* 1278) was writing three-part counterpoint in the thirteenth century. But good as his work is it does not attain the level of the Reading Roto.

almost without challenge, for some four hundred years.

The difficulty of estimating our mediæval music is greatly enhanced by the imperfection of the record. Our popular music was not written down at all —there was no one to write it. Of our ecclesiastical music the chant alone was transcribed on fair parchment; the accompanying parts were intended only for the choir, and were entrusted to miscellaneous scraps of parchment or of paper, which were soon scattered and mislaid; the score was a mere memorandum for the composer, and was destroyed as soon as it had served its purpose. There is no known manuscript of any musical score until the seventeenth century: all compositions before that time were either unwritten or left to the hazard of the part-books. Even these were often at the mercy of some reforming abbot or precentor who disapproved of their licence and either sent them to the bookbinder or consigned them to the rubbish-heap. A vast number of them have been irretrievably lost, a few are gradually being recovered by the labours of devoted scholars who have ransacked the corners of libraries and the dusty shelves of practice-rooms, and have pieced together the mutilated fragments into some kind of coherence.

One example of such restoration, which it is appropriate to mention here, is the volume called *Worcester Medieval Harmony*, compiled and edited by the scholarly care of Dom Anselm Hughes.[1]

[1] Plainsong and Mediæval Music Society, 1928. The other volumes of this admirable series are invaluable to students of the period.

The See of Worcester had inherited a love of Church music from the time when Dunstan was its bishop: the fruits here collected amount to no less than 101 compositions of the thirteenth and fourteenth centuries, gathered from the libraries of Worcester Cathedral, the Bodleian, the British Museum, and Magdalen College, Oxford. Many of them are short, some are incomplete, all are anonymous, but they bear witness to a definite school of Church composition which until recently was altogether unknown. It is not claimed that they possess the high value of the Reading Rota: genius like that is a rare and royal visitant; but they maintain throughout their course a level of sound workmanship and sincere feeling which gives them an assured place in the history of our liturgical music.

During the latter half of the period to which they belong the cause of musical scholarship was being advanced by Walter Odington, a monk in the neighbouring Abbey of Evesham, whose treatise, *De Speculatione Musice*, elucidates many of the points that are illustrated in their practice. Indeed all across the chart of our early music we find as outposts the contributions made to musical science by British and Irish writers. Earliest of these was Alcuin, who left York to teach in the schools of Charlemagne; later came John Cotton, whose treatise was long ascribed to no less an authority than Pope John XXII; then John Garland, scholar, schoolmaster, and crusader, who helped to found the University of Toulouse, and who not only commented on the principles of music but exemplified them in his own compositions; the so-called " Anony-

B   E.M.

mus of the British Museum," who was a monk at
Bury St. Edmunds, and who has left us some of the
most significant allusions to the English music of
the fourteenth century; and Walter Odington,
greatest among them all, who seems to have known
everything comprised in the musical erudition of
his day. It is our loss that these learned men were
too closely confined within their study walls to
bestow much attention on the more human aspects
of the art, that they were mainly occupied with
grammatical precepts and rules of formal punctilio.
We would not, perhaps, resign anything that they
have to teach us; but we sometimes wish that they
had found leisure to visit the earl's banqueting-hall
or the village green on a feast-day and had brought
back some record of their impressions. However,
they were not different, in this matter, from their
Greek predecessors, or their French and Italian contemporaries; and the importance of what they have
given to scholarship makes us disinclined to com-
plain of what they have withheld.

For in spite of official reticence there is beginning
to emerge from the darkness a new radiance of
secular music. We had not in England such splendid
organizations as those of the Troubadours and
Trouvères in France or the Minnesingers and
Mastersingers in Germany: as we were leading
their nations in the Church so we fell behind them
in the court and the market-place. But there have
come to light a good many "songs and madrigals"[1]

---

[1] A collection of these was published by the Plainsong and
Mediæval Music Society as long ago as 1891. See also *Early
Bodleian Music* by Stainer and Nicholson.

of the fifteenth century, not only carols, in which
the period is particularly rich, but songs of a more
secular character. Good examples are to be found
in the Selden manuscript, which is dated by scholars
between 1415 and 1455, and which, beside carols and
sacred pieces, includes a spirited drinking-song, a
lyric in praise of country life, and what may well be
regarded as the climax and cynosure of them all, the
superb song of thanksgiving for the victory at
Agincourt.[1] It is one of the finest popular tunes in
the world, a noble Triumphlied in which the
patriotism of a nation speaks out of a full heart.
George Brandes once said that Shakespeare's
Henry V was a national anthem in five acts. The
Agincourt song is its compendium and quintessence:
a core of white heat that burns in the very soul of
our people.

So the scene unfolds itself with its alternations of
light and shadow, of soloist and chorus, and the
time has come when a chief actor shall make his
way forward and take the place of pre-eminence that
has been prepared for him. The fame of John
Dunstable has been somewhat overwhelmed by the
fanfare of praise with which some writers have
heralded it: the trumpets are so insistent that we
cannot hear the voices of welcome. Responsible
historians have attributed to him the "invention of
counterpoint," and have built on this astonishing
sentence a theory not less astonishing that England
in the fifteenth century was the origin and cradle
of organized musical composition. It should be
unnecessary to say that Dunstable no more "in-

[1] See Illustration B.

vented counterpoint" than Bach invented the fugue
or Handel the oratorio. Nc one invented counterpoint, it grew out of the natural varieties of the
human voice, and to assign its earliest known
practice to the fifteenth century is, as we have seen,
an anachronism of over five hundred years. But
Dunstable was its greatest exponent who had yet
appeared: as pre-eminent in his generation as Bach
or Handel in theirs.[1] We may perfectly well accept
the tradition that the Flemish composers who came
nearest to rivalling him—Dufay, for example, and
Binchois—were either pupils in his school or
disciples under his influence: indeed Martin le
Franc, writing in 1437, says plainly that these two
men

>Out prins de la contenance
>Angloise et ensuy Dunstable
>Pour quoy merveilleuse playsance
>Rend leur chant joyeux et stable,

and Johannes Tinctoris, the saturnine Flemish critic,
who does not like England or English ways, ascribes
the whole progress and development of musical
composition throughout the century to a group of
composers "quorum caput Dunstable extitit."[2]
Assuredly he was recognized by his contemporaries
in Western Europe as a master of those who know.
   Yet of his biography we are completely ignorant.
We have only the date of his death, 1453, and a

---

[1] See Illustration C.
[2] Preface to his volume entitled *Proportionale Musices*. It is not
dated, but must have been written after 1476, *i.e.* at least forty years
later than the poem of Martin le Franc.

couple of epitaphs, one by Abbot Whetamstede, which extol in colloquial Latin his command of the four quadrivial sciences—arithmetic, geometry, astronomy, and music. His name appears to have been soon forgotten in their country—it is not even mentioned by Bale, and its recovery at the end of the nineteenth century indicates by sheer extravagance the degree of our previous neglect.

We English have a remarkable gift of forgetting our great men, but an oblivion so deep as this calls for some attempt at explanation. One hypothesis has been suggested—that Dunstable may have left home in early life and accomplished the chief part of his work on the continent. He may well have found England an uncomfortable abode for an artist. If we accept 1370 as the conjectured date of his birth, which there is reason for doing, the two chief events of his boyhood were the Peasants' Rising which devastated the southern counties and captured the Tower, and the systematic persecution of the Lollards, which condemned England, as Mr. Trevelyan says, to a hundred years of intellectual stagnation.[1] His early manhood was contemporary with a civil war, his later with the miserable bickering and misrule which culminated in the Wars of the Roses. It would not be surprising if he had felt that the spear was being too often lifted against the Muses' bower, and sought for relief in voluntary exile. To this may be added an important, though indirect, piece of positive evidence. Of the fifty

---

[1] Trevelyan, *History of England*, p. 249. "No single act," he adds, "had more to do with the barrenness of English mental and spiritual life in the fifteenth century."

compositions definitely ascribed to Dunstable hardly
any have been discovered in this country. There are
three in the British Museum, there is one at Old
Hall in Hertfordshire, all the rest, which an exhaus-
tive search can reveal, are from Continental collections, mainly at Trent and Modena. The natural
inference is that they were written not in England
but in Austria and Italy, and this conclusion is
further strengthened by the known inter-relation
which took place in the fifteenth century between
English and Italian scholars. Padua, Ferrara,
Florence, and Bologna were in particular visited by
English students, and among them it is not unreasonable to suggest that Dunstable found a place,
and that he left to this adopted region the legacy of
his maturest work.[1]

Martin le Franc gives as the two chief qualities
of Dunstable's music, sweetness of tone and firmness
of outline. In both these he surpassed all that we
know of the music of his contemporaries: beside
him even the great Flemings—Dufay and Binchois
and Okeghem—seem to shine by reflected light. It
is not until Josquin des Pres, in the next generation,
that a star of similar magnitude rises above the
horizon. For expressive melody and for control of
the dialogue of vocal parts he was in his time
unrivalled, and after all our centuries of advance and
invention we may still confirm the judgment that
places him among the *Di majorum gentium.*

[1] The Trent manuscripts of Dunstable have now been removed
to Vienna and edited by the Gesellschaft zur Herausgabe der
Tönkunst in Oesterreich. The Modena manuscripts have been
edited by the Plainsong and Mediæval Music Society.

One of his larger compositions, the motet, "Quam pulchra," may be consulted in Grove's Dictionary[1]—others are illustrated in Walker's *History of Music in England*,[2] others in the second volume of the Oxford History, and others in the interesting paper contributed by Ch. Van der Borren to the transactions of the Musical Association.[3] Perhaps the most penetrating account of his work is that of Dr. Guido Adler,[4] who played so great a part in the collection and publication of the Trent Manuscripts. As an indication of the charm and mastery of his writing we may take the opening of the song, "O Rosabella," now in the Vatican.[5] And on its transparent and expressive melodies we may conclude the most chequered and elusive period of our musical history.

[1] Third Edition, vol. ii, p. 112.
[2] pp. 23-25.   [3] 15th March 1921.
[4] *Handbuch der Musikgeschichte*, pp. 250 seq.
[5] *Vide* Appendix C.

CHAPTER II

THE TUDOR PERIOD, I AND II

IT will have been observed that all our English music, from Dunstan to John Dunstable, is and remains anonymous. The attribution of the Reading Rota to John of Fornsete is purely conjectural— apart from it there is not even the material for conjecture. This was no doubt in the fashion of the age: we do not know the names of our earliest English poets except Aldhelm, Caedmon, and Cynewulf; we do not know who designed the fabric of Durham Cathedral; we do not know who painted the rood screen of Hexham or who illuminated the Bedford Book of Hours. In these days of strenuous advertisement it is hard to realize a time when artists worked not for themselves but for their craft, when they were too modest to claim even the just recognition of their achievements, and when they would as soon have thought of selling their autographs as of appending them to the staves of a motet or the pages of a missal. The change began about the middle of the fifteenth century. After that time, no doubt, we have still some anonymity and some mis-attribution, but the stream was finding its outlet by the year 1450, and it was set in its course by the greatest of our musicians. When he added "Qd. Dunstable" at the foot of an enigma canon he made an innovation as drastic in its way as that of Ben Jonson, when some hundred and sixty years later he challenged opinion by publishing his dramas.

Where Dunstable led the way, lesser musicians were not slow to follow, and the practice of personal attribution may be fully exemplified in the Old Hall Manuscript[1] dated a few years after his death (*c.* 1460 or later). This most important document, which belongs to the College of St. Edmund, Old Hall, near Ware, contains 138 sacred compositions of which the vast majority are ascribed by name to English composers—twenty-four in all. They are possibly the members of a school, not the masters, and not all equally proficient, but all of great interest as indicating the general course and level of English Church composition. Most of the names have no great claims to remembrance, a few rise above the prevailing mediocrity. Lionel Power, to whom no less than twenty-one pieces are ascribed, was a younger contemporary of Dunstable's, and has left some reputation both as composer and as theorist. Damett is noticeable for a motet to St. George, which is in many ways typical of the polyphonic structure of the time. It is in the usual three parts: the treble sings a hymn in six-line stanzas to the honour of the Virgin; the alto or "mean" a second hymn, with different words and music, to the honour of St. George, and the tenor supports them both with a chant in long, protracted notes, of which the only words are "Benedictus" and "Maria."

[1] For description of this MS. see articles by W. B. Squire in the *Journal of the Internationale Musikgesellschaft* for 1900-1, p. 342 seq., and by Sir Richard Terry in the *Monthly Musical Record.*

This method, while accentuating the freedom of the part-writing, did not make for clearness in the understanding of the text: it led, as we shall see later, to a serious abuse in the next generation.[1]

But among all the contributors the most historically interesting is King Henry VI—Roy Henry—whose Credo and Sanctus give evidence of high musical attainment.[2] We may pause here to observe the effect on English music of royal patronage and example, and this not only in one period alone but almost throughout its history. Richard Cœur de Lion was as great a minstrel as Taillefer. Henry V held his chapel in such favour that he summoned it to attend him at Rouen during the French War. Henry VI was one of the first Church composers of his day. Edward IV established a permanent gild of musicians, and supported it with munificent bounty. Richard III remodelled the services of the Chapel Royal; Henry VII relaxed his habitual parsimony to uphold their prestige; and so the roll continues with Henry VIII and Mary and Elizabeth, and the later dynasties which will be recorded in their due place. This outburst of royal munificence was followed and even matched by some of the wealthier nobles and corporations. In the sixteenth century, for example, the houses of Buckingham and Northumberland maintained large musical establish-

---

[1] This form, technically known as the motet, goes back as far as the Troubadours and is habitually employed in the secular motets of Adam de la Halle. See Coussemaker's edition of his Works, especially the end of the Introduction.

[2] The sanctus is quoted by Woodridge (*O.H.M.*, vol. ii, pp. 151-2), who also quotes in the same chapter examples of Dunstable, Power, Damett, and Pycard.

ments; so did Cardinal Wolsey, so did Magdalen College, Oxford.[1] Indeed by the time of the madrigalian era, English composers could look as confidently for patronage as could those of France and Austria in the eighteenth century.

The inclusion in the above list of an Oxford college leads us to consider the part played by music in the educational system of the time.[2] By common consent it was given a place among the sciences of the quadrivium; it was always held in favour as an amenity of social life. The former gave to its severer aspects an assured place in all Church schools and colleges; the latter made its lighter graces an essential part of the pleasures of Court and castle. And because the universities were the meeting-places of erudition and social amenity they were much noted at the time for their encouragement of music and musical practice. As we shall see later they were both prominent in the careers of some of our most celebrated Tudor composers. Shortly after the death of Dunstable they showed their sympathy with the art by conferring upon it the distinction of a Musical Degree. The earliest recipients of whom we have record were Thomas Saintriste, Provost of King's College, Cambridge, who took

[1] See Davey, *History of English Music*, pp. 77-82.
[2] The mediæval system of formal education classified its subjects in two divisions. The first, called the Trivium, comprised the three elementary sciences of Grammar, Logic (or Dialectic), and Rhetoric: the second, called the Quadrivium, comprised the more advanced studies of Music, Arithmetic, Geometry, and Astronomy. This distinction which goes back to Martianus Capella in the fifth century was embodied in a couple of mnemonic verses—
Gram. loquitur: Dia. vera docet: Rhet, verba colorat:
Mus. canit: Ar. numerat: Geo. ponderat: Ast. colit astra.

his Doctorate in 1463; Henry Abyngdon, Master of the King's Music, who took his Baccalaureat about the same time; John Hamboys of Oxford, who belongs also to the reign of Edward IV, "an excellent musician," says Hollinshed, "and for his notable cunning therein made Doctor of Music"; and above all Robert Fayrfax, who took his Doctorate in 1501, and with whom the full light of our Tudor music may be said to dawn.

Some forty years after the Old Hall Collection, that is to say, about 1500, there appeared another document of even greater value and importance. This was the Eton Manuscript, originally compiled for the College chapel, and now preserved as a chief treasure in the College library. It is said to have contained ninety-seven compositions, and though that number has been sadly depleted by the ravages of time, there still remain over forty examples for investigation. The composers chiefly represented are Cornyshe, Fayrfax, Banaster, Richard Davy, and Thomas Wilkinson, the transcriber of the whole series; their music consists mainly of motets, in four, five, and six parts; magnificats of similar elaboration, and a noble though incomplete setting of the Passion by Richard Davy. Four of the pieces are by Thomas Wilkinson, who must have been a contrapuntist of remarkable attainment, for one of his contributions is a Salve Regina in nine parts, and another a canonic setting of the Apostles' Creed in thirteen. An interesting pendant to the Eton Manuscript is a so-called Antiphonarium, of a somewhat later date, which is now in the Advocates' Library at Edinburgh, and the rediscovery of which we owe, as we owe so much else in our knowledge of mediæval music, to the researches of Dr. Fuller Maitland.[1] Its very list of contents is significant, "a round dozen of Masses, thirty motets, and six settings of the Magnificat," and it carries the command of polyphonic resource to a point far beyond any that had been reached at its time either in England or on the Continent. The only composer mentioned by name is Robert Carver, Canon of Scone, who was born about 1491, and was therefore contemporary with our early Tudor period. His name is attached to several compositions, among others a Mass in ten parts and a motet, "O bone Jesu," in no less than nineteen, the latter of which is constructed on a plan of unprecedented scale and elaboration. This motet has been transcribed by Dr. Fuller Maitland and is therefore generally accessible; further works of Robert Carver are now finding their way into the choir-books of Westminster Cathedral;[2] and of other "places where they sing." We are in process of restoring to its due dignity the reputation of this great forgotten master.

E tribus disce omnes. The three manuscripts above cited, even if they stood alone, which they do not,[3] would sufficiently refute the commonly accepted charge that our music, after Dunstable, went through an interval of decline and degradation. The

---

[1] See his article in Grove, vol. i, p. 574.
[2] Father Long, master of the choristers at Westminster Cathedral, has (1930) transcribed four Masses, including the "Dum Sacrum" in ten parts, together with a Kyrie and a Motet "Invenerunt me." One of the Masses, for three equal voices, is a continuous flow of melody.
[3] See the list of other collections in Davey, *op. cit.*, pp. 87-102.

fact is that our historians have allowed themselves
to be browbeaten by Johannes Tinctoris and have
accepted his unfavourable verdict without any
sufficient examination of the evidence. It is time to
carry the case to appeal, on the ground of mis-
direction. The Flemings, he says, are always
adventuring into new paths of song: the English,
"quod miserrimi signum est ingenii," plod along a
beaten track without invention or variety. The first
half of this sentence we can cordially welcome as
true—Flemish music at this period was beginning
to lead the world—but there is neither reason nor
justice in using it as a stick for beating Englishmen.
We may well admit that the composers of the Old
Hall Manuscript show a certain timidity and con-
servatism: they were not the successors of Dunstable but his lesser contemporaries. The composers
of the Eton Manuscript and the Edinburgh Antiphonarium did to some purpose "adventure into
new paths of song." They made valuable experiments towards the defining of musical form, and
even towards the redistributing of balance and proportion among the constituent parts, so far as is
consistent with contrapuntal freedom.[1] They were
consummate masters of technical resource, and it
must be remembered that in the early stages of an
art the invention of technique may be itself a mark
of genius: for technique becomes wearisome only
when it becomes imitative. They equipped music
with a new sonority, a new fullness of texture, which
should serve as a garment for the greater genius

[1] See Dom Anselm Hughes' paper on the Eton MS., Mus.
Ass., 27th February 1927, p. 70.

that was soon to come. They were forerunners and preparers of the way, but they did much more than plan out its course: so far from hindering the advance they bore in it a useful and honourable share.

This is apparent when we come to consider the earliest group of our Tudor composers. They were touched no doubt by Flemish influence—there had long been intercourse between the two countries—but they were not overwhelmed by it: they had their own message to deliver and their own discoveries to communicate. The chief names among the group are those of Fayrfax, Cornyshe, Aston, and Redford: composers who though too diverse in aim to constitute a school have this in common, that with them the claims of secular, dramatic, and instrumental music begin to find a larger and more official recognition than had yet been accorded to them. All were born in the fifteenth century, all completed their work by the middle of the sixteenth, and they are of sufficient standing in history to merit some separate and individual treatment.

To Fayrfax (1465-1521) allusion has already been made in our account of the Eton Manuscript. He was primarily a Church musician—choir-master of St. Alban's and gentleman of the Chapel Royal—but he seems to have taken a hand in the Court pageants, accompanied Henry VIII to the Field of the Cloth of Gold in 1520, and was so notable a writer of secular songs that one of the chief miscellaneous collections of the time is known as the Fayrfax Book. This divided allegiance has its effect on the style of his Church composition. He is not so skilful a

contrapuntist as are some of his predecessors, the
curve of the moving parts is sometimes a little stiff
and reluctant, but he has a real sense of dramatic
contrast and colour, and he is at his best when he
forsakes intricacies of decoration and piles up his
structures into large and stately volumes of sound.
He left six Masses—seven if the Missa "O quam
suavis" can be attributed to him,[1]—together with
sixteen motets, a few settings of the Magnificat, and
about a dozen secular songs of various character:
a thin harvest for remembrance but of great historic value. And we may observe that Antony à
Wood, writing a couple of hundred years later, can
still speak of him as "in great renown and accounted
the prime musician of the nation."

A more substantial figure to us, is William
Cornyshe, who was born about the same year and
died in 1523. He also was a member of the Royal
Household and a Gentleman of the Chapel Royal,
but his talents were of a different order and his
career in a different field. Under Henry VII he seems
to have followed a somewhat chequered course—in
1504 he was sent to the Fleet for writing a pasquinade
—but Henry VIII took him into high favour, made
him Master of the Court revels, and even accepted
his advice and collaboration. He had a natural gift
of satire and a natural sense of comic construction:
the former found its outlet in his setting of Skelton's
breathless invective, the latter in the fashioning of
pageants and interludes of which he was as great

[1] See Mr. Collins' edition of this Mass, in the *Transactions of the
Plainsong and Mediæval Music Society*. The probable date of the
Mass is about 1500.

a master on one side as his contemporary, John Heywood, on another. The music of these is lost, and we can judge them only by their contemporary reputation. But the range and variety of his songs is enough to establish his fame as a lyric composer. Twelve of these are included in a sumptuous volume (British Museum, Add. MSS. 31,922), which probably belonged to Henry VIII, and contains several songs attributed to the royal hand; three more of first-rate importance are in the Fayrfax Book; four more, of which the bass parts alone survive, were printed by Wynkyn de Worde; and they touch the chords of many emotions—tender as in "Ah! the sighs," and "Adew Corage," bluff as in "Blow thi horne hunter," satiric as in the Skelton songs, convivial as in "Hoyda jolly rutterkin." Our English music of later times has been conspicuous both for tenderness and for humour; we can find them abundantly in the writings of this sixteenth-century artist.

With Hugh Aston (1485-1522?) another side of musical composition comes into prominence—the development of instrumental music as an independent art "to which people were expected to sit and listen." Hitherto there had been no record that the music of instruments could be used for any purpose except to accompany the voice or keep time for the dancers' feet, and we came near to claiming a real invention when Aston wrote his "Hornpipe for Virginals"—a dance measure in name, in reality an elaborate virtuoso piece which almost anticipates the jewel work of Byrd and John Bull. And if we can attribute to him the authorship of "Lady Cary's

C   E.M.

Dompe,"[1] he is the first known composer to employ the variation form, of which so abundant a use is made in Parthenia and Queen Elizabeth's virginal book.

The place of Aston's birth was long a matter of controversy, but is now determined as Mawdesley, in the county of Lancashire. He took his M.A. at Oxford in 1507, migrated the same year to Cambridge; by 1509 was Canon of St. Stephen's, Westminster; and by the end of his life, Archdeacon of York.[2] His surviving Church music consists of two Masses and six motets, three of which are unfortunately incomplete: strong and dignified writing which does not stand out very saliently from the better Church music of his time. But it is by his adventure into the unknown land of instrumental music that his reputation is established, and that on the strength of two compositions, one of which is conjecturally assigned. No artist ever attained immortality with so small an offering.

Yet the immortality is not ill-bestowed, for there is hardly any discovery in music the consequences of which have been more far-reaching. Aston's Hornpipe is the ancestor of a long succession of masterpieces for harpsichord and clavichord[3] and piano-

---

[1] The Hornpipe and the Dompe were both published by Stafford Smith in his *Musica Antiqua*, 1812.

[2] The evidence for identifying Hugh Aston with the Archdeacon of York is given in the Carnegie *Tudor Music* edition, vol. x, Introduction.

[3] Virginal, spinet, and harpsichord are three species of the same genus, a keyed instrument in which the strings are plucked by a quill. The clavichord was a much smaller keyed instrument in which they were pressed by a brass tangent. But in the fifteenth century the name clavichord was often indifferently used for the whole of both genera. See *Oxford History of Music*, vol. v, pp. 55-6.

forte—the fugues of Bach, the sonatas of Beethoven, the fantasias and capriccios of Brahms—the family has spread throughout the civilized world, and has found fortune in its most distant regions. A consequence, not less momentous than the main issue, is that the introduction of the virginals into the full comity of music extended the venue of the art from the Church and Court to the more friendly intimacies of the home. Aided by an improvement in the construction and use of the viols, it rapidly brought encouragement to music in the domestic circle, and to it may be attributed in some considerable degree the advance of skill and taste which came to permeate every corner of English society.

Meanwhile organ-building in England had considerably improved upon its early method. Wulfstan, a contemporary of Dunstan, has left us the description of his organ—four hundred pipes, forty slides, and twenty-six bellows with seventy blowers. The splendour of it is so great, he adds, that every one within reach has to stop his ears, "being in no wise able to draw near and hear the sound." (It will be remembered that Aelred in the twelfth century condemns the organs of his day for noise and dissonance.) These primitive instruments were played with slides, like the tops of domino-boxes, which it required considerable vigour to manipulate: and conditions were not much ameliorated when these were replaced by a keyboard, since each key was five inches wide and took the whole weight of the performer's fist. But every generation softened the asperities of its predecessor, bringing about an

easier action and a greater variety of tone and compass, until by the sixteenth century it had become
possible to treat the organ as a solo-instrument and
to give it an independent voice in musical discourse.
So in the fitting time came John Redford (1486-
1540), a younger contemporary of Aston and the
first in the succession-line of our famous organists.
He was a man of wide and versatile ability—first
one of "Paule's boys"; then their choirmaster and
arranger of the school plays; then occupying a
similar office at St. George's and the Chapel Royal,
where he brought his actors up to a pitch of excellence which came at last to excite the jealousy of
grown-up performers. When Rosencrantz complains to Hamlet of the "aery of children, little
eyases that cry out on the top of question and are
most tyrannically clapped for 't" he is re-awakening
the echoes of a long controversy which even in his
time had not ceased from troubling. Besides these
activities Redford was well known as a writer of
morality plays, both words and music, one of which,
Wyt and Science, attained a great vogue and reputation. His choral works for the Church are neither
numerous nor important, though it may be mentioned that his anthem, "Rejoice in the Lord," still
holds a place in our service-books. But he is chiefly
to be celebrated as the first known writer of organ
voluntaries, some twenty of which, copied by a later
choirmaster of St. Paul's, are now in the British
Museum. They do not as yet show any special sense
of organ-technique, indeed they appear to be
transcriptions of motets, the names of which they
still bear. Their main interest lies in their recogni-

tion of organ playing as an independent form of art, treated as Orlando di Lasso later treated the viols when he marked some of his madrigals as "buone da cantare e suonare "—"apt for viols and voices."

It may be well to summarize here the progress of English song, up to the point at which we have now arrived. One of the great beauties of our early literature is the clearness and freshness of its lyric poetry. "Lenten is come with love to toune," "Wynter wakeneth al my care," "Alysoun," "The Lover's complaint," and many others which must as a matter of course have had their musical counterparts. The stream once set flowing never ran dry. Carols and hymns, aubades and lullabys, love-songs, and songs of the countryside, these abound in every generation and vie with one another in sweetness of expression and daintiness of form. The lyric, "Of on that is so fayr and bright," may be called the loveliest of mediæval hymns, but little below it is "Adam lay y-bounden, bounden in a bond," with its touch of delightful if conscious artifice. About the same time comes, "I have twelve oxen," each verse of which ends with the refrain:

"Sawyste not you mine oxen, you lytyll prety boy."

Later follow songs of Christmas festivity like the "Boar's Head" and "The Holly and the Ivy," songs of religious fervour like "I sing of a mayden" (another gem of pure loveliness), songs of romance like "Walsingham," songs in praise of good ale, and meditative songs of which the best-known is

"Pastime with good company," by King Henry VIII. Many of them are religious, some of the others apologize for their secularity by some modification or extension of the words; thus the famous lyric, "Come o'er the burn, Bessie," which is quoted by Shakespeare, has in the Fayrfax book an allegorized second stanza in which Bessie is mankind and is summoned to cross over the confines of the world within which she has been held captive. But these are of rare occurrence. The gift of lyric song, regarded at first, perhaps, with some ecclesiastical misgiving, grew in strength and freedom of utterance as the nation advanced, until with Fayrfax and Cornyshe it chanted its prelude to the Elizabethan age.[1]

The second group of Tudor composers is a Pleiad of seven stars: Taverner and Shepherd, Tye and Merbecke, White and Parsons, and Farrant.[2] With these men we enter into a more familiar region: three of them have been fully reprinted in the Carnegie edition, others are represented in Barnard, and have so found their way into current use: we still sing every Christmas a hymn tune adapted from Tye; Merbecke's setting of the Creed is still the most habitual, as it is the noblest, in our service-books; we still set the Magnificat to "Farrant in G minor,"

[1] About thirty of our fifteenth and sixteenth century song-melodies are quoted in the chapter "Henry VII to Mary" of Wooldridge's *Old English Popular Music*. All are of distinctive character: many are of great charm and beauty.

[2] Walker (*History of Music in England*, p. 48) would add William Mundy, but I do not feel that we know enough about him. He is chiefly celebrated as composer of the anthem, "O Lord, the Maker of all thing," which was long attributed to Henry VIII.

and welcome among our Anthems "O praise God in His holiness," and "Lord, for Thy tender mercies' sake." The language of music is coming to anticipate more closely our modern idiom: and it may be taken as an analogue that English is beginning first to rival and then to replace the use of Latin in our Liturgy.

In the history of this group the strangest career was that of John Taverner (*c*. 1495-1545). Born and brought up in Lincolnshire, he was at an early age appointed to the living of Tattershall in that county, and is said to have written almost the whole of his music there before he was twenty-five. On the establishment of Cardinal's College at Oxford he was recommended to Wolsey as master of the choir, and after some demur and hesitation (he wanted to get married and the College statutes were a hindrance), his difficulties were overcome and in 1526 he entered upon his new office. This, which would have been the beginning of most musical careers, was the end of Taverner's. The College was "a hotbed of Lutherans," and amid their ranks he found salvation. In 1528 he was, with several of the Fellows, accused of heresy, and escaped the general disaster on the disdainful ground that he was "only a musician." Shortly afterwards he resigned or was dismissed from his organistship, transferred his allegiance from Wolsey to Thomas Cromwell, expressed contrition for his past errors, and at one step turned his back upon the whole of his previous life. From 1538 he was actively employed in the suppression of monasteries and friaries through the north of England especially in his native county, and his letters to

Cromwell indicate that he was carrying out his duties with all the barbarous and persecuting zeal characteristic of the time. He had evidently become a person of high political importance, and it is probable that he retained his position until the downfall of his patron in 1540. But there is no evidence that he wrote a line of music after his departure from Oxford at a little over thirty years of age.

His works, which are astonishingly virile and mature, include eight Masses and forty smaller works for the Church—motets, magnificats, and other settings of devotional texts. Of these the Masses are the most important (though the lesser volume contains the famous Leroy Kyrie), and it is in relation to the greatest of them that a point of Church musical practice may here be discussed.

The earliest Masses were chanted to unaccompanied plainsong, and the successive numbers— Credo, Gloria, and so on—were treated as isolated units. The growth of polyphony suggested a means of interrelating them; a piece of plain song was taken as staple which ran through the entire texture, and round which the accompanying parts were woven. From this it was an easy step to the adoption as staple, or *canto fermo*, of some great hymn melody— "O quam suavis," or "Æterna Christi Munera"— much as Bach in later times fashioned his Church cantatas round the chorals of the Lutheran office. And then the practice turned down a by-path which was as dangerous as those in *The Pilgrim's Progress*, and came as near ending in disaster. Many secular songs of the time had melodies which were not only beautiful and striking but eminently suited for contrapuntal treatment: some of these were taken over and employed in the Mass service, so that the voice which held the *canto fermo* was singing a tune associated with love or wine during the very act and process of worship. The most popular of these —a French or Provençal ditty called "l'Homme Armé"—was so used by more than twenty eminent composers, including Dufay, Busnois, Josquin des Pres, Morales, and Palestrina.[1] The practice came to England from France or Flanders, and was soon adopted: our most salient examples being the Masses of Taverner and Shepherd and Tye on the beautiful and passionate melody of "Western Wynde."[2]

There is no evidence that the words of the secular song were used in addition to the music. If they were they could not have been heard in that welter and confusion of speech which roused Erasmus to condemn Church music as violating St. Paul's injunction against speaking in an unknown tongue. It is also arguable that the tunes were not undignified, and that at this lapse of time they sound to us as little incongruous as Innsbruck or the Passion Choral. But when all allowances are made the practice did not tend to edification. Everybody in the congregation knew the tune, everybody was accustomed to connect it with associations which were not always respectable and a text that was not always decorous. It may be that the public forgot its associations and surrendered itself to the impressions

[1] A Kyrie on this tune is to be found among the works of Robert Carver.
[2] See Illustration D.

of the moment. It may be that, like our modern Protestant congregations, it took no notice of the matter, one way or the other. At any rate the method which began under high sanction and authority came to be noted as an abuse, and led to those reforms which so narrowly saved Church music at the Council of Trent.

But if the custom calls for defence it could have no better advocate than this Mass of Taverner. The tune, one of the finest in our sixteenth-century treasure-house, appears in each number with hardly any alteration or embellishment, running through the texture like a gold thread in a brocade, distinct from the rest, yet enriching them all. To discuss its merits in detail would lead us further into technicalities than befits the present volume: enough to say that it speaks with the true accent of poetry, elevated in thought, pure in style and, in the command of its material, unfaltering.

Like many of our sixteenth-century Masses, Taverner omits the Kyrie altogether,[1] and mutilates the Credo with a cut from "Whose Kingdom shall have no end" to "and I look for the resurrection of the dead." These defects, or at any rate the latter, impair their liturgical use and may help to explain the disregard into which they have fallen. But as

---

[1] Out of forty-two Masses examined by Wooldridge and Arkwright only eleven contain a Kyrie, and seven of these form a set specially composed for Henry VIII's Chapel. The probable explanation is that the Kyrie was often set as a separate composition which could be transferred from one Mass to another. For the omission of words from the Credo no explanation can be given except sheer carelessness, a carelessness which mars, in almost the same place, the Credos of Schubert.

examples of distinguished and eloquent art they and
his other works are well worth reviving: they fully
deserve the fine tribute paid to him by his most
recent editors:

> "Relatively he sums up all the qualities of his
> predecessors and contemporaries and expresses all
> their ideals. . . . Absolutely his mastery of a most
> intricate idiom and his amazing vitality and virility
> place him among the world's great composers. [1]

In strong contrast to the career of Taverner is the
quiet, smiling, uneventful life of his next contemporary. John Shepherd was born in the early years
of the century and educated at St. Paul's under
Mulliner, the enthusiast who copied out, *manu
propria*, the organ voluntaries of Redford. In 1542
he was appointed choirmaster of Magdalen College,
Oxford, and held that office intermittently for five
years when he was promoted to a Fellowship.
Some time later he was a gentleman of Queen
Mary's private chapel—presumably organist—and
the only other known facts of his biography are that
in 1554 he supplicated for the degree of Mus. Doc.,
"having occupied twenty years in the study of
music," and that about 1563 he died. His works
include four Masses, one on plainsong, and one on
"Westron Wynde," several anthems, of which three
were published by Day and one by Barnard, a large
number of motets, and four pieces with accompaniment for lute, the first appearance of that

[1] Carnegie Edition of *Tudor Church Music*, vol. i., Introduction,
p. xxiv.

instrument in our English annals. Unfortunately many of the motets are incomplete—the tenor is wanting from the part-books—but enough remains to show that he had not only a great command of form, but a most remarkable skill in part-weaving. The motet "Esurientes" which is quoted by Burney (*History*, vol. ii, p. 583), is a masterpiece of ingenuity and design; we may hesitate to endorse the judgment that it shows him to be "superior to any composers of Henry VIII's reign,"[1] but it is without doubt a credential which made him free of the company.

A stronger claim for supremacy may be made on behalf of Dr. Christopher Tye (*c.* 1500–*c.* 1573), whose masterful personality kept him in continuous office through the political and religious vicissitudes of four reigns: who wrote Masses under Henry VIII, who set the Acts of the Apostles in the new Protestant style for the use of Edward VI, who was possibly music-master to Queen Mary and was probably an organist of the Chapel Royal to Queen Elizabeth. Yet there was nothing in him of the time-server: he stood far too firmly on his feet to be shaken by any winds of doctrine, and the same superb confidence which made him give the name "Euge Bone" to one of his own Masses continued to the end of his life when he met Queen Elizabeth's rebuke that he was "playing out of tune" with the audacious answer that the fault was in the ears of Her Majesty.

He was east-country born and educated at Cambridge, where in 1536 he proceeded to the

[1] Burney, vol. ii, p. 565.

degree of Mus. Bac. and to that of Mus. Doc. in
1545. Shortly after the establishment of the Bishop-
ric of Ely he was appointed organist and choirmaster of that cathedral, and remained in office
until 1561, when he was, characteristically enough,
succeeded by his son-in-law, Robert White. He had
already taken orders and been instituted to the
Rectory of Doddington (where he is described as
"having no special aptitude for preaching"): he
presently added to this the further livings of
Wilbraham and Newton. It is regrettable to add
that two of these were sequestrated on his refusal to
pay the first-fruits.

His place in the history of music is due partly to
the high reputation which he enjoyed,[1] partly to the
opportunity afforded him by the course of public
events in Church and State. One result of the
Reformation in England was the insistence that the
services should be given in a tongue understanded
of the people. This meant not only translation of
the text from Latin to English, it implied also the
use of a more transparent music through which the
words themselves should be clear and articulate.
So when in 1544 there appeared an English version
of the Litany, Cranmer took the occasion of sending
to Henry VIII a drastic letter on the subject of its

[1] Henry's estimate of him is expressed in a quotation, probably
authentic, given in Rowley's "When you see me you know me,"
where Prince Edward says:

> " I oft have heard my Father merrily speake
> In your hye praise, and thus his Highnesse sayth
> England one God, one truth, one Doctor hath
> For music's art, and that is Doctor Tye."

musical setting. The music, he enjoined, was to be plain, not florid, not "full of notes," but "as near as may be for every syllable a note, so that it may be sung distinctly and devoutly." And the same principle is reaffirmed in those visitations of King Edward VI to which in great measure we owe the form of our English prayer book. It must not be supposed that the change took place all at once, or that it was ever universal. For one reason, the old methods had taken deep root in the affections of the country: for another Latin is pre-eminently well fitted for musical treatment and the gain in clearness was qualified by a loss in ease and flexibility: for another, and this the most significant of all, many of our Tudor composers were and remained staunch Roman Catholics who, whatever advantage they might take of new methods, had no intention of forgoing their old allegiance or their old polyphony. At the same time it is true that Cranmer's reform upheld a new method and opened a new field for its exercise. From it may be dated the great vogue of the English anthem, the comparative simplicity of the English service, and, in its insistence on note-for-note harmonies, the gradual evolution of the English psalm-tune.

Tye, who was graduating at Cambridge when Cranmer's letter appeared, came in on the wave of the new movement. He had already shown his mastery of polyphonic resource—his Mass "Euge Bone" deserves all the praise that has been bestowed upon it—and it is probable that some of his Latin motets belong to the post-Reformation period; but in his Acts of the Apostles he broke fresh ground and introduced into music a simple forthright narrative style which is a landmark in the history of the art. Still more notable are his anthems, three of which are to be found in Barnard and some fourteen of which survive to the present day. They are still enriched with some of the contrapuntal dignity of their inheritance, but they are full of suave and beautiful sound and they are typically English in feeling. Two examples of his "direct, homely, almost popular" melody are made generally accessible by Wooldridge:[1] better known and loved is the exquisite "Lord, for thy tender mercies' sake," which, long misattributed among his contemporaries, may now with reasonable confidence be assigned to him.[2] He is the first English Church composer who appeals directly to the affection and sympathy of the nation at large and with him, as Walker says, "popularity was never inconsistent with musicianship of a kind that is among the permanent glories of the English school."[3]

Of the other three masters a less detailed notice may suffice. Robert White (*c.* 1535-1574) was the son-in-law of Tye, graduated at Cambridge in 1560, and held successively the organistships of Ely, Chester, and Westminster Abbey. He seems to have written almost entirely to Latin texts, indeed his only known English compositions are four anthems, and one of these, "O praise God in His holiness," is said to be, in both of its forms, an

---

[1] *Oxford History of Music*, vol. ii, pp. 342-350.
[2] Dr. Fellowes assigns it to the elder Hilton. But the internal evidence for Tye is very strong.
[3] *History of Music in England*, p. 42.

adaptation of an earlier unspecified work. His chief Latin works are two settings of the Lamentations, in which, after a tradition which even Palestrina followed, the words *Incipit Lamentatio* and the names of the Hebrew letters are treated with the same expressive care as the verses themselves. Beside these are some very remarkable motets, of which the most conspicuous are the "Miserere," the "Exaudiat te," and the third "Dominus quis habitabit." He was a past master in the art of canonic imitation and device: indeed the intricacies of "Dominus quis habitabit," particularly of its last number "Ad nihilum deductus," are not surpassed in their kind until the most mature scholarship of the seventeenth century.[1]

Of more intimate significance to Englishmen (for White has been sadly neglected) is John Merbecke (*d. c.* 1585), who was a singing-man at Windsor in 1541, and in 1543 was arrested with three of his fellow lay-clerks on suspicion of Calvinistic heresy. The trial took place in 1544, the other three were condemned, and Merbecke owed his acquittal to the personal intervention of Gardiner, on the ground apparently that he was too good a musician to be sacrificed. In 1550 he gave a more acceptable proof of his Protestant leanings by publishing *The Booke of Common Praier noted*, a setting of the Liturgy which would have delighted the heart of Cranmer. Much of it was superseded by the changes in Edward's second book (1552), but his version of the Nicene Creed remains, and it may be hoped will always

[1] All his known works are published in Vol. V of the Carnegie *Tudor Music* edition.

endure, as the fitting musical embodiment of our confession of faith. This was Merbecke's one great contribution to liturgical music. Four Church compositions (one of them imperfect) are printed in vol. x of the *Tudor Music* edition, and it is noticeable that the first of these is a Mass. But Merbecke early withdrew from his musical pursuits, though he seems to have retained the organistship of Windsor, and devoted himself henceforth to Biblical and theological studies, among which a concordance and a set of controversial pamphlets are sufficient evidence of his uncompromising Protestantism.

Robert Parsons (*d.* 1569-70), was a native of Exeter, and was sworn Gentleman of the Chapel Royal in 1563. The slenderness of his achievement is explained by the fact that he died prematurely, drowned in the Trent at Newark: it includes three services (one printed by Barnard), a few anthems, and motets, a madrigal, and some pieces for viols, full of delicate skill and adventurous harmonic colour. One work of his which raises him to the rank of master is an "Ave Maria" in which the treble maintains a *canto fermo* rising through successive notes of the scale and the other voices weave an accompanying texture of moving parts. It may almost be claimed as the ancestor of Bach's figured chorals and it is hardly less beautiful.

Last in this category comes Richard Farrant (*d.* 1580), who was a Gentleman of the Chapel Royal under Edward VI and resigned this post in 1564 to become master of the choristers at Windsor. In 1569 he was reappointed to the Chapel Royal, and fulfilled both offices together until the time of his death. Among his duties it fell to present an annual play to the Queen, and we have the names of at least two in which he wrote songs for solo voice with string accompaniment. His most famous pieces of Church music are the service commonly called "Farrant in G minor" (though the oldest version of it appears to be a tone higher), and the two delightful anthems, "Call to remembrance" and "Hide not thou thy face." He is one of the most attractive figures in this middle period, a period which is beginning abundantly to exchange promise for achievement, and it is pleasant to pass upon his name to the greater and fuller glories of which he was a harbinger.

CHAPTER III

THE TUDOR PERIOD, III

IT is at first sight remarkable that in this difficult time our Church composers succeeded in retaining not only their heads but their offices and reputations. The course of strict orthodoxy was devious and obscure, the way was beset with pitfalls on either side, the penalties for transgression were usually drastic: yet these men, the chief part of whose work lay within the precincts, seem to have been given a freedom which was certainly not enjoyed by the country at large. Taverner and Merbecke, as we have seen, fell into some peril of the law: both were acquitted. Tye transferred his allegiance to the Anglican use, White maintained his preference for the Latin, yet both alike occupied their public position unchallenged and unmolested. Even more striking were the fortunes of Tallis and Byrd. Tallis was organist of Waltham Abbey at the time of its dissolution in 1540: he was at once appointed by Henry VIII to a similar post at the Chapel Royal, and held office there continuously until his death, at an advanced old age, in 1585. Byrd, who succeeded him, was to the end of an equally long life a convinced Roman Catholic, the greater part of whose writings were ostensibly for the Roman service. No doubt he is said by an over-credulous traveller to have "sacrificed everything for his religion—both his office and his hopes of preferment"; but there is no evidence that he ever sacrificed anything, unless we so regard an occasional fine of one shilling for his wife's absence from church: the cheque-book of the Chapel Royal makes it quite clear that with all his avowed Romanism he retained his appointment.

Two reasons may be suggested. One is that Henry and Elizabeth were both artists: the one was himself a composer and took active part in the Court revels, the other was an expert performer on the virginals who readily forgave an indiscreet ambassador on his assuring her that she "played better than Mary Queen of Scots." It was natural that they should keep in their hearts a sympathy with fellow-musicians, that they should view their pursuits with favour and their transgressions with lenience.[1] The other is that with both monarchs the doctrinal issue was subordinate to the political. Henry was a learned theologian, but his prime article of religion was that "the Bishop of Rome hath no jurisdiction in this Realme and Impire of England." Elizabeth was a devout Protestant but, as she frankly told the Catholic Earl of Worcester, she was more concerned with her subjects' loyalty than with their religious tenets. And we may remember that Pope Clement VII had mortally quarrelled with Henry over the question of the divorce, and that Pope Pius IV had declared Elizabeth illegitimate, and had

[1] Sebastian Westcote, organist of St. Paul's, was confirmed in his office, though an avowed Romanist, "quod tam carus Elizabethæ fuit."

absolved her subjects from their allegiance. It was no time to divide England with religious controversy when the timbers were being cut for the Spanish Armada.

Be this as it may, the two colleagues who brought our English music up to its highest pinnacle of glory wrought equally for the Roman Catholic and the Anglican Liturgies. Their biographies are largely conjectural—we know as much on the subject as we are ever likely to know, and for this we are indebted to the minute researches of scholars such as Mr. Barclay Squire, Mr. Jeffrey Pulver, and above all Dr. Fellowes, who has made himself the chief living authority on Elizabethan music. Even they can tell us little or nothing about Tallis's early life. The year of his birth may have been anything from 1505 to 1510—probably not later. He may have been educated at St. Paul's School—there is no record. The first date that emerges with any certainty is 1540, when he was transferred from Waltham Abbey to the Chapel Royal. In 1547 he received his livery for the coronation of Edward VI, and in 1552 he married. Of his wife we know only that her name was Joan, that she survived him, and that he "lived with her in love full three and thirty years." We may date at about this time the beginnings of his friendship with William Byrd, of whom he was first the teacher[1] and afterwards the close and intimate colleague, an association which may without extravagance be compared with that of Haydn and

[1] Wood says definitely that Byrd was " bred up to music under Mr. Tallis," and these words are corroborated by a laudatory poem prefixed to the Cantiones Sacræ of 1575.

Mozart. Tallis was considerably the elder of the two, and at the time of their meeting was the most famous musician in England: Byrd was the more brilliant and adventurous, a disciple who in sheer force of genius was greater than his master. One difference is salient enough: Mozart died at thirty-five, Byrd continued to scale height after height until he was eighty. But the friendships while they lasted were as close in the one case as in the other, and almost as momentous.

Tallis was high in favour with Queen Mary, who in 1557 granted him, as special reward, the lease of a manor in the Isle of Thanet. Queen Elizabeth continued the Royal bounty with a grant of £40 (about £500 of our money) in the first year of her reign. It was possibly in acknowledgment of this that he printed his first published work, a collection of anthems which appeared in the *Certaine Notes* of John Day from 1560 onwards. He had been writing anthems as far back as 1547: it is significant that his first publication of them should follow so closely after a signal example of Protestant patronage.

In 1572 Byrd joined him at the Chapel Royal, and in 1575 the two colleagues obtained from Elizabeth a patent for the printing and selling of music-paper. As a means of livelihood this was not successful: both the partners were musicians without business experience and one of them was nearly seventy years of age: within a couple of years Byrd complained that they had lost 200 marks by the transaction, and they were glad to call into alliance the more practical abilities of Thomas Vautrollier. But it gave them the opportunity, which they readily welcomed, of publishing some of their own compositions, and the result was a volume of *Cantiones Sacræ*, sixteen motets by Tallis and eighteen by Byrd, which appeared in 1575 and which while it confirmed the reputation of the older artist permanently established that of the younger. This was the last known work of Tallis. Shortly after it he resigned his post at the Chapel Royal: he spent a few years of honourable retirement at Greenwich, and there in 1585 he died.

William Byrd (1543-1623) is said to have been born in Lincolnshire and educated, like so many of his contemporaries, at St. Paul's School. He had evidently some good general education, for we find him later on giving lessons in mathematics to Thomas Morley, and writing letters in forthright and fluent Latin: his musical reputation is early attested by his appointment, at the age of nineteen, as organist of Lincoln Cathedral. In 1569 he was sworn a Gentleman of the Chapel Royal: in 1572, on the appointment of his successor at Lincoln, he migrated southward with his wife and children and took up his residence first at Harlington in Middlesex, and then at Stondon Place near Ongar. He was granted the leases of two manors, both of which cost him some litigation: apart from this and an occasional dispute with his Archdeacon he seems to have lived in charity with all men: if he was sometimes glanced at as a "Popish recusant," he had powerful friends who could turn the point of the arrow: he enjoyed the continuous friendship of courtiers and statesmen: by his fellow artists he was regarded with no less affection for his character than admiration for his genius.

The true biographies of both men lie in the record of their compositions. In dealing with these some lines of demarcation are easily drawn. There is no evidence, for example, that Tallis wrote anything of importance after 1575, so that the end of his career virtually coincides with the beginning of Byrd's. Again Tallis wrote almost entirely for the Church, and preferably for the Roman use: Byrd, in addition to his lavish abundance of Church music, composed over a hundred madrigals and secular songs and over a hundred and fifty instrumental pieces. In spite therefore of their twin greatness we may take them separately and begin with the category which they have chiefly in common.

It is probable that the bulk of Tallis's Latin Church music was written while he was at Waltham Abbey: at any rate the two Masses, the two Magnificats, and the two settings of passages from the Lamentations. The motets are as landmarks all through his career, and the finest of them are among those which he contributed to the *Cantiones Sacræ*: such noble examples as "Absterge Domine," "Candidi facti sunt," "In jejunio et fletu," and, best of them all, "O sacrum convivium." He writes by predilection in four or five parts: two of his motets are in six, and one (the date of which is unknown) in forty. This amazing piece of technical (and more than technical) skill is laid out for eight choirs of five voices each, singing now antiphonally, now altogether; it is as complex as the most modern orchestral score, and it flows onward to a concluding issue which, though of course restricted by the laws of pure vocal counterpoint, is an ocean of moving and voluminous sound.[1] As a rule Tallis's music has little intricacy, little involution; it is strong, simple, dignified, caring more for solidity of structure than amenity of decoration. The "Miserere," with its elaborate descant, is an exception: the common plan of his architecture is Norman—even Romanesque—rather than Gothic. And though his English Church music is on the whole inferior to his Latin, we have some fine anthems of his, apart from the adaptations; and we cannot forget that we owe to him our most familiar setting of the Preces and the Litany and two of our best-beloved hymn-tunes.

His death in 1585 left Byrd the undisputed monarch of English music, the annals of whose beneficent reign occupy a space of forty years. In 1588 came the *Psalms, Sonets, and Songs of Sadness and Pietie*, thirty-five compositions dedicated to Sir Christopher Hatton and prefaced with the well-known manifesto in praise of singing. Next year followed another collection of forty-seven compositions, entitled *Songs of Sundry Natures*, and in 1591 the second and third volumes of *Cantiones Sacræ*, which by themselves entitle him to a place among the great masters. To this time also belongs the first of his three superb Masses, the finest of their kind ever written by an English composer, and of the highest rank all the world over. Not Lassus or Palestrina ever rose to a loftier and more serene eminence. With them closed for the time a period

[1] It can be seen in the Carnegie Edition of *Tudor Music*, vol. v, pp. 299-318.

of strenuous activity, and was followed by an interval of silence and meditation. At the end of this he returned, bringing as fruits of solitude the two volumes of *Gradualia*—one hundred numbers in all— which were published in 1605 and 1607 respectively, and which many critics have acclaimed as his supreme masterpiece. Even these did not exhaust his indomitable vigour. His second and third Masses are assigned to 1610, his book of *Psalms, Songs, and Sonets* to 1611; two years later, at the age of seventy, he contributed four anthems to Leighton's *Teares and Lamentations of a Sorrowful Soule*: then he laid aside his pen and wrote no more. His death, in 1623, is notified in the records of the Chapel Royal as that of a "Father of Musicke": in the time of our greatest achievement he stands among all his contemporaries supreme and unrivalled.

For comparison with Tallis we are to take here only his sacred compositions—the secular and instrumental works will come to description later. Their very number is surprising: three Masses, over two hundred motets and other Latin pieces, several important contributions to the English liturgy, and eighty-five anthems. And in all this array there is no example of slovenly design or hasty workmanship. [1] It is usually held that among the Masses the five-part is the best; and this, if we must express a preference, is probably correct, though it contains

---

[1] This is not to advance the absurd opinion that all his work is of equal value. Every artist finds at times that his invention has flagged—if a man were always at his best he would have no best, and Byrd is no contravention of this law. But it may be confidently maintained that his noblest work is of untold value, and that few composers have fallen so seldom below their highest level.

nothing finer than the Sanctus of the Mass for three voices,[1] or the Credo and Agnus Dei of the Mass for four. Among the motets it is as hard to make a selection as among the cantatas of Bach: the reader who is making their acquaintance may well begin with the brilliance of the six-part "Hæc Dies," the splendour of "Exsurge Domine," the nobility of "Tu es Pastor ovium," the deep pathos of "Ne irascaris,"[2] and the intimate devotional feeling of "Justorum animæ." Chief of his English works is the Great Service, vast in scale and magnificent in conception: among the anthems may be specially noted "Praise our Lord, O ye Gentiles," "Sing joyfully," "O Lord, rebuke me not," "How long shall mine enemies," and the chorus "Rejoice, rejoice," from the Christmas music. In some of these anthems Byrd intersperses the choral section with solos, concerted pieces, and even short interludes for the organ: an innovation which both widens the variety of their structure and enhances the poetry of their expression.

It was on this aspect of his art that Byrd laid his chief insistence. A complete master of technical resource—and his motet "Diliges Dominum" is perhaps the most astonishing canon in existence— he is not less conspicuous for the insight with which he fits his music to the text. The light of this ideal had scarcely dawned on previous Church composers: at most they had made some general distinction of

---

[1] See Illustration E.
[2] The second section of this "Civitas sancti tui" has been adapted to English words, and is known as "Bow Thine ear" to many of our choirs and congregations.

sad and joyful music without any great care for
exact propriety of detail: the same strain had done
duty for Kyrie and Credo, for Gloria and Agnus
Dei, and, as we have seen, the words themselves
were often obscured by the tangled web of polyphony. From this error Byrd did more than any
other musician to liberate us. With him the significance of the words came first, and the melodies
came chiefly to enforce and interpret them.

"There is," he says, "a certain hidden power
in the thoughts underlying the words themselves:
so that as one meditates upon the sacred words
and constantly and seriously considers them, the
right notes, in some inexplicable manner, suggest
themselves quite spontaneously."[1]

This from the man who was the most learned
contrapuntist of his day, and who realized that
learning itself was of avail only as the handmaid of
inspiration.

We may trace this ideal through almost every
page of his compositions: the splendid range and
opulence of his melody; the audacities of his harmonic colour, which so shocked the pedants of the
nineteenth century and which have proved to be so
certainly and triumphantly right; the depth and
sensitiveness of his emotion; his variety of structure,
always adventurous and always suitable to the

---

[1] Dedicatory letter to Lord Northampton prefixed to the first
volume of the *Gradualia*. See Fellowes, *William Byrd*, pp. 27-28.
It is noticeable that Byrd is here speaking of the Latin text: the
English follows *a fortiori*.

subject proposed. Much of his music is exacting in performance; it demands not only a wide compass of voices, but a keen and responsive intelligence. Yet we have come to see that no labour can be too great to make us worthy recipients of the inheritance that he left us. The stupid neglect which consigned him to oblivion for nearly three centuries has now and for ever passed away: his rediscovery has unveiled for us the noblest and most sublime monument of our national music.

The Church music of Orlando Gibbons belongs to the next chapter. Of Byrd's other contemporaries Thomas Weelkes wrote some fine anthems, but all alike won their renown in the fields of secular and instrumental composition. Chief among them were the madrigalists, who are sufficiently numerous and sufficiently cognate to be regarded as a definite school. With the problems, philological and historic, which surround the name madrigal we are not here concerned[1]: enough to say that from 1533 when a famous collection was published in Rome, to about 1630 when the name gradually passed out of usage, it was applied to secular songs in three or more independent parts, clothing lightly and easily a great diversity of subjects. Many of them are love-songs, pastorals of swains and shepherdesses, others are meditative or sportive, satiric or epigrammatic, following the humour of the poet wherever it led. One will take for its theme the pangs of despairing passion, another the arrival of

---

[1] They have been fully treated by Dr. Fellowes (*English Madrigal Composers*) and Professor Dent (Grove, vol. iii, pp. 275 seq.), who have done much to clear up a difficult question.

Morris-dancers at a country fair; one is in a tone of courtly compliment, another is a cynical complaint that the people of England are "mostly fools." In its stricter definition the earlier stanzas of the madrigal were set to the same music and the last, usually repeated, clenched the whole on a different strain; in general acceptance this rule was often relaxed and a wide freedom accorded to poet and composer.

For about thirty years the leading places in this art were taken by Flemings, French, and Italians. England entered the field about the mid-century: a delightful example by Richard Edwards, "In going to my naked bed," is dated 1564, and is as true a madrigal as anything in Arcadelt or Marenzio. We were indeed well suited for carrying on the tradition. For the madrigal was essentially a domestic form of music, not a matter of public display—there were no concert-rooms in Europe—but for honest pleasure and recreation in the home: and not only are we the most home-loving of nations, but we were at that time the most widely equipped in musical skill and knowledge. Erasmus, who knew many men and cities, has no hesitation in assigning to us the first place: by the end of the century our musical culture was so widely diffused that it was taken for granted. A well-known illustration is the sad case of Philomathes in Morley's *Plaine and Easie Introduction*, who is asked at supper to decide a knotty point of musical criticism, and after supper to take his part in a madrigal; and the centre of the story is not his discomfiture at failing, but the total inability of the company to believe that it is genuine. When after

long argument he convinces them that he has really
"no skill at these numbers," they break into wondering groups, inquiring among themselves, "where
he had been brought up." And the extent to which
this percolated through every rank of society may
be attested by one of Robert Green's traits in which
a common adventuress describes her education:

> "After I grew to be six years old," she says,
> "I was set to school, where I profited so much
> that I writ and read excellent well, played upon
> the virginal, lute and cithern, and could sing
> prick-song (*i.e.* staff notation) at the first sight:
> insomuch as by that time I was twelve years old
> I was holden for the most fair and best qualitied
> young girl in that country near London."

Our culture has in many ways improved on that
of the sixteenth century: we have still something to
learn from an age in which an understanding of
musical æsthetics was taken as part of a gentleman's
equipment, and in which a child under twelve could
sing complicated music at sight and play passably on
three instruments.

But we have no need to call isolated witnesses:
we have only to open our Shakespeare in order to
see how thoroughly English life was saturated with
the love and skill of music. The exceptions prove the
rule. Othello "does not greatly care to hear
music"; Hotspur would rather hear his brach howl
in Irish than Lady Mortimer sing in Welsh; but
around them the isle is as full of voices as was ever
Prospero's kingdom. Desdemona sings of her

sorrows and Ophelia of her passion; the courtiers
in Arden join in their songs of sport and of philosophy; Sir Andrew Aguecheek, who "plays the viol-
de-gamboys better than any man in Illyria," takes
his quavering part in a catch; Silvia is celebrated in
one of the loveliest of serenades; it is through the
concourse of sweet sounds that Lorenzo woos
Jessica and Viola soothes the melancholy of Orsino.
And at the other end we have the clowns with their
snatches of broken melody, the shearers by the sea-
coast of Bohemia "three-man song-men all and very
good ones, but they are most of them means and
basses"; Falstaff sends out for "Sneak's noise"
(which is a less disparaging term than it appears),
and the Athenian homespuns end their entertainment
with a Bergamask. Shakespeare has little to say
about painting and sculpture: music is the art which
lies at the centre of his affections, as it did with those
of his countrymen.

In his description of Hengrave Hall Dr. Fellowes
has given us a charming account of the equipment
and routine of a great Elizabethan house.[1] The day
began about 6.30, and the morning was occupied
by the men in field sports and by the women in
housekeeping, reading, or embroidery. The dinner
hour was usually about twelve, and the afternoon
spent in the garden or the bowling green or the
tennis court if the house were opulent enough to
possess one. After supper, which took place about
5.30, the company diverged, some to cards and dice,
some to the singing of madrigals or the support of

---

[1] See his volume on the English Madrigal, Part 1. The rest of
the book is equally valuable to students of the subject.

the voices with a "consort" of viols, or to solos with
the accompaniment of lute or cithern, or to the
virginals, which by the end of the century were
coming into high favour among virtuosi. Occasionally perhaps the range might be further extended.
We find mention among the Hengrave instruments
of a curtall, two "sackboots," and a lysarden,[1]
beside other forerunners of the orchestra. And the
household music was under the direction of "Master
John Wilbye," the most renowned madrigal
composer of his day.

The madrigals were printed not in score but in
part-books which usually consisted of four sheets
lying head to head in the shape of a cross, so that
the singers could stand round a small table and find
each his own part under his eyes. No one, therefore,
could see what his neighbour was about, or gain
any assistance from a survey of the general effect:
there were no bars or expression-marks, there was
of course no conductor, and to keep one's place
must have required a considerable measure of skill
and experience. The singing may not have been
always of high quality—it was not intended as a
concert-show—but its very prevalence is an indication of the widespread pleasure which it afforded.

The vogue of the madrigal may be dated in
England from 1588. In that year Nicholas Yonge,
a London merchant who had close dealings with
Italy, published a volume of Italian examples, under

[1] A curtall was a small bassoon, a sackbut was a kind of trom-
bone, a lysarden that queer, tortuous instrument of wood and
leather which under the name of "serpent" survived in some
village bands up to the time of Thomas Hardy.

the title of *Musica Transalpina,* and as a special compliment to an illustrious fellow-countryman included in it two settings by Byrd of Ariosto's *La Virginella.* From that moment the fashion spread with a rapidity which can be paralleled only by the vogue of the English sonnet. Over seven hundred and fifty madrigals have been discovered and catalogued, apart from settings of Biblical texts. They represent the work of more than fifty composers. When in 1603 Thomas Morley published the *Triumphs of Oriana,* a collection of madrigals in honour of Queen Elizabeth, twenty-six musicians contributed and every work is a masterpiece. Even the great Italian collection, on which it was modelled, does not show such high and sustained excellence.

To the *Triumphs of Oriana* Byrd for some unknown reason did not contribute. But his mastery of the form is evident both from the number and the quality of his examples in it. He is most intimately at home in its serious vein: in such instances as "Retire, my soul," or "Why do I use," or "Come, woeful Orpheus," with its extraordinary audacities of modulation; but he can relax on occasion into a lighter mood as in the famous "Amaryllis" madrigal which used so to baffle our nineteenth-century conductors, or "This sweet and merry month of May," or "I thought that Love had been a boy," which is as gay and humorous as a ballet of Morley. They have been overshadowed, and perhaps justly, by his writings for the Church: they would have established the reputation of many composers.

Four more madrigal writers are of conspicuous importance. The eldest is Thomas Morley (1558-

1603), a pupil of Byrd, a collaborator with Shake-speare, editor of the *Triumphs of Oriana,* and author of that delightful text-book the *Plaine and Easie Introduction.* He was organist successively of St. Paul's Cathedral and of the Chapel Royal, but his chief bent was for secular music, especially in its lightest and most attractive form. His whole published work falls within the space of four years, from 1593, when he commenced author at the age of thirty-five, to 1597, when his career was closed by failing health. During that time he printed about a hundred concerted pieces, some of which he called canzonets, some ballets, and some madrigals: a genial, lovable personality who served his generation with a cheerful heart, and has endeared himself to ours with such gifts as "Now is the month of Maying," "My bonny lass she smileth," and the admirable comedy of "Hark! jolly shepherds," and "Ho! who comes here?" We have been so much concerned with Melpomene and Polyhymnia that we welcome Thalia and Terpsichore with something like relief.

The other three men were almost exact contem-poraries: Wilbye was born in 1574, Weelkes in 1575, and Gibbons in 1583. Wilbye we have already met as director of the music at Hengrave Hall, to which office he was appointed about the time that Morley began publication, and in which he remained until the breaking-up of the establishment in 1626. He then migrated to the home of Lady Rivers, a daughter of the house who seems to have been his special patroness, and spent there the last twelve years. Among our madrigal writers he holds by common consent the first place. He published two volumes, in 1598 and 1609 respectively, and the sixty-four examples which they comprise include such imperishable masterpieces as "Alas! what a wretched life is this," "Adieu, sweet Amaryllis," with its lovely reconciling close,[1] "Oft have I vowed," as full of poignant emotion as it is of technical skill, and the two most widely beloved of all Elizabethan madrigals, "Sweet honey-sucking bees" and "Flora gave me fairest flowers."

We owe it partly to our national temperament, partly to our isolated position, that English music at this time stood looser than her continental neighbours to customary laws and prohibitions. The system of mediæval modes, for example, while providing a language of great purity and dignity, closely restricted the range of harmonic colour; and this prevailed longer on the Continent than in this country.[2] Little by little our composers, especially the madrigalians, began to relax their bonds, so arose a new feeling for modulation and for chromatic harmony, until by the end of the period we were virtually discarding the modes and merging them into the larger freedom of the major and minor scales. In this advance the most adventurous pioneer was Thomas Weelkes, organist first of Winchester College and then of Chichester Cathedral, whose madrigals (there are ninety-nine in all) were published between the ages of twenty-one and thirty-three. They are, in fact, a young

[1] See Illustration F.
[2] The Prince of Venosa may be cited as an exception. But he stands, so far as I know, alone and in any case he proves too much.

man's work—he apologises in the first volume for his "unripened years"—and they are marked by all the freshness and audacity of youth. Among the most notable of them are assuredly examples of *nuove musiche*. "Cease sorrows now," which has been described as "the finest three-part madrigal in existence," contains a passage in canon on a rising chromatic scale: "O care thou wilt despatch me," is a remarkable instance of free modulation for emotional or picturesque effect, and the opening of its second number, "Hence, care, thou art too cruel,"[1] may be described in modern language (there was no language for it at the time) as a juxtaposition of cadences in remote keys, as novel and startling as that of the Sanctus in Beethoven's first Mass. Oddly enough these experiments alternate with periodic returns to orthodoxy. "As Vesta was from Latmos hill descending" is in the accustomed manner, possibly because it was written for the *Oriana* volume. "Your beauty it allureth," in which he seems to move with less ease than usual, is a pure example of modal counterpoint; but though he kept open a door of refuge he wandered farther afield than any of his comrades and brought back treasures the existence of which they hardly suspected.

Gibbons (1583-1625) is chiefly famous as a composer of anthems: indeed his sole store of madrigals is comprised in a single volume which he published in 1612. His prevailing tone is grave and solemn, as though with him the madrigal caught some echo from the Church service: he has keen feeling for expressive melody and harmonic beauty of sound,

[1] See Illustration G.

and his place is assured by "the Silver Swan," "Dainty fine bird," and the fine austere setting of Raleigh's "What is our Life?"

The vast bulk of Elizabethan vocal music was concerted, but a special word should be said on the solo-songs which towards the end of the period came more and more into usage. We may indeed trace the very frontier line of transition. Dowland, writing in 1597, says that he has composed his songs "in four parts, so made that all the parts together or either of them separately may be sung to the lute, orpherion, or viol-de-gambo." Campian, writing in 1601, has shifted the balance. His songs, he says, are in the first instance for the solo voice, adding that "upon occasion they have been filled in with more parts which whoso pleases may use, who likes not may leave." Of the others Rosseter wrote by preference for the solo voice, Ford, Robert Jones, and Pilkington for either method indifferently.

John Dowland (1563-1626) was a famous lute-player who travelled widely as a virtuoso, through France, Germany, and Italy; and who in 1598 was appointed lutanist to the Danish Court with ministerial rank and salary. He not unnaturally complains of the contrast between his welcome abroad and his neglect at home: but Elizabeth was growing old, James I was but a sluggish patron of the arts and it was not until 1612 that some amend was made by the offer of a post in the King's household. By his fellow-artists he was held in high esteem, and his praises were celebrated in Barnefield's famous sonnet on music and poetry which takes him as representative of the one art and Spenser of the

other. As a song-writer he was in his time without
a rival and we can still listen with delight to " Awake,
Sweet Love" and "Now, oh now, I needs must
part," and other "melodious ayres" which through
the lapse of many generations have lost no whit of
their charm and fragrance.

Next both in time and in rank is Thomas Campian
(1567-1619), a London doctor who won even
greater fame as a poet than as a musician. Indeed
about half the lyrics in his first volume were set by
his friend Philip Rosseter: four other volumes
appeared at intervals and in these also his music
is set to his own words. His poems are of a very
high order—we have but to cite "Rose-cheeked
Laura," "Follow your saint," and "Never weather-
beaten sail" to give illustrations. His music is the
exact counterpart, simple, tuneful and transparent,
suiting the exact declamation of the phrases and
echoing its thought with melody which if never
deep is always sincere and spontaneous. The
remaining song-writers are of less account to us:
they "twine their white violets," like Meleager, into
the wreath of poetry; yet for sheer pleasure we may
recall with gratitude the dainty stanzas of "Sweet
Kate," or "Since first I saw your face," or "Have
you seen but a bright lily grow?"

The accompaniment was usually assigned to lute
or viols. The former was shaped like the half of a
pear and set with catgut strings which varied in
number according to the size,[1] and which were

[1] Some of the different kinds of lute are depicted in Grove,
vol. iii, p. 252. For the notation of lute-music see the article on
Tablature in Grove, vol. v, especially pp. 249 seq.

plucked with the finger. Its tender and delicate tone made it a supreme favourite in Elizabethan society; it was "as much part of a gentleman's accoutrements as his sword"; it hung on the wall of every drawing-room for the solace of waiting visitors. But its great merits were compensated by a sensitive and capricious temper; it required constant tuning, and was so expensive in broken strings that according to a current jest it cost as much to keep a lute as to keep a horse. In the hands of Shakespeare's Katharine it must have exhausted a small fortune. We may note with interest that this drawback does not seem in any degree to have diminished its popularity.

The viols,[1] ancestors of the violin family, were bowed instruments with flat backs and normally six strings, gentle and sweet in tone, and much employed in concerted music. For this purpose they were commonly arranged in sets (called technically "chests" or "consorts") which contained two each of their customary sizes—treble, tenor, and bass. They had far less brilliance and agility than violins, which at first emergence were regarded in England with some disfavour, but they were eminently well suited to their object, and their revival at the present day, by the skill and enthusiasm of Mr. Arnold Dolmetsch, has done much to improve our knowledge and strengthen our appreciation of Elizabethan music.

Some of the other instruments in use we have already found among the recorded inventories of Hengrave. A considerable number are named in the

[1] See Grove, vol. v, p. 514.

fourth song of Drayton's *Polyolbion* where the
English, challenged by the Welsh to a contest of
music, advance to the fray with a formidable
armoury of weapons. Some of these, like the
"pandore," became obsolete in a little more than
a generation: some like "hoboy" and "shaum"
have survived in a modified form up to the present
day. It is noticeable that Drayton does not mention
trumpets or drums: these were kept for special
occasions of pageantry and would have been
regarded by the artists of the time as arrogant and
blustering intruders. For it must be remembered
that there was then no such thing as an orchestra
in England. Some primitive attempts were made at
combinations of different instruments—Bacon in
the third "century" of his *Silva silvarum* makes a few
interesting suggestions on the point—but these were
significantly known as "broken music" and had
little vogue and little effect. The art of contrasting
and associating various *timbres* was yet in its infancy,
and was still confined within its nursery walls.
Queen Elizabeth's "band of forty" was no more than
a glorified fanfare: the incidental music of the theatre
consisted of half a dozen players in the musicians'
gallery, and was so little prearranged that the
audience treated it as a joke and called at will for
"Greensleeves" or "John, come kiss me now," or
some other ditty of the streets. The Church and the
home were the two shrines in which music was
honoured: outside them it had to shift for itself.

Yet in one important respect the cause of music
as a whole was aided by the growth of instrumental
practice and proficiency. This was the improvement

and development of dance-forms. It is clear that in every rank of society dancing was a popular amusement, and the taste for it encouraged a growth of melodies which had a remarkable influence on the subsequent history of the art.

The first known collection of dances came to us from France: the *Orchésographie* of Thoinot Arbeau, Canon of Langres, which appeared in 1589. We followed, a few years later, with Anthony Holborne, who in 1597 published an instruction book for the cithern, containing some examples in dance measures, and supplemented it in 1599 with a volume entitled *Pavins, Galliards, Almains, and other short Airs, both grave and light, in five parts for Viols, Violins, or other musical wind-instruments*. It is in some ways an elusive book. There are no bars, no indications of speed, and no essential differences of style to distinguish the thirty dance-tunes from the thirty-five other pieces which are designated as songs and some of which are to sacred words. But it is of great value as indicating the kinds of dance which were chiefly in fashion among our Elizabethan forefathers and illustrating them with examples.

The three of most musical account are those which he names in his title. The Pavan (not "the Peacock dance" but "the dance from Padua") was a grave and stately measure in common time with smooth and flowing melody and much ceremonial movement; the Almain, also in common time, was more elaborate, more "full of notes" and as became its German origin, more erudite in construction. Arbeau tells us that it was "becoming antiquated in

France," but we were more conservative and more tenacious. The Galliard, which Shakespeare calls "nimble," was a merry, sprightly dance in triple time, the gambols of which were regarded with some disfavour by precisians, but which were very popular as an opportunity for gymnastic display. "I did think from the excellent constitution of thy leg," says Sir Toby, "that it was born under the star of a Galliard," a challenge to which Sir Andrew unhesitatingly responds.[1]

Many other dances are mentioned by Shakespeare,[2] the Measure, "full of state and ancientry," the coranto, swift and running, the breathless jig, the cinque-pace with its five steps and its curious halting rhythm. And while we gave full welcome to these foreign visitors, and adorned them with our own music, we were keeping in market-place and village green, our native stock of country dances, both the name and the character of which are wholly English.

At first the dance tunes were simple and artless, fulfilling their purpose in the movements which they accompanied. But as time went on and executive skill increased, the composer's invention kept pace with it and the melodies became such as could be heard in their own right with growing interest and pleasure. So it became customary to join two or more of them together as concert-pieces, and, for the sake of artistic contrast, to select those which showed a marked difference of style or expression.

[1] *Twelfth Night*, I, ii, 143.
[2] See Beatrice on "Wooing, wedding, and repenting." *Much Ado*, II, i, 72.

As early as 1597 Morley recommends the alternation
of Pavans and Galliards, and this proposal was no
doubt encouraged by Anthony Holborne's volume
two years later. Hence came the first germinal
beginnings of the suite, an organized system of
instrumental pieces which culminated in the cognate
forms of Sonata, Quartet and Symphony. And
even at this early period we may carry the story a
stage farther. Byrd who among his many innova-
tions gave, in some of his later motets, a "speaking
part" to the strings, published in 1613 a six-part
Fantasia for viols, which is not an adaptation of
motet or madrigal but an independent composition
for instruments alone. And with it the history of
concerted chamber music may be said to begin.

During this period, and especially towards its
close, there was also a great advance in the construction and use of organs. A famous builder was
John Chappington, who in 1597 made the organ
of Magdalen College, Oxford: another, even more
celebrated, was Thomas Dallam, whose "handsome
double-organ" was erected at King's, Cambridge, in
1605 and is said to have given a moment's inspiration to Shakespeare.[1] Other organs mentioned with
commendation are those of York, Durham, Lich-
field, Hereford, Bristol and Exeter; indeed the only
noted exception is that of Carlisle which a dis-
contented traveller compared to a "shrill bagpipe."[2]

About the organ-music of the time we know little

[1] It was famous all over England for the depth and sonority of
its bass: and may well have suggested Alonzo's comparison of the
thunder to a "deep and dreadful organ-pipe" in *The Tempest*,
III, iii, 97.

[2] Grove, vol. iii, p. 749.

or nothing. Churches and cathedrals almost certainly restricted it to the uses of the service; its lay-substitute was the regal, a small portable instrument employed on occasions of special solemnity. But the case is far different when we come to the music of the virginals which spread far and wide through the country and almost rivalled in consideration, if not in amount, the prevailing ascendancy of song and madrigal. The first collection of virginal pieces engraved in England was *Parthenia,* which appeared in 1611: a set of twenty-one numbers, eight by Byrd, seven by Bull, and six by Orlando Gibbons: others which followed are Ladye Nevell's book (forty-two pieces), Will Forster's book (seventy-eight), Benjamin Cosyn's (ninety, with some Church music added), and the Fitzwilliam Virginal Book, compiled but not published in the early seventeenth century,[1] which gathers a full harvest of over four hundred compositions. The predominant writer is Byrd: the whole of Lady Neville's book is by him and he appears most frequently in that of Will Forster; but a round score of English masters are represented; among them Mundy, Tomkins, Peter Philips, and Giles Farnaby, the last of whom contributes some of the most beautiful numbers in the collection. The contents are made up largely of dance measures, with some general pieces such as Preludes and Fantasies, some queer anticipations of descriptive music, and some sets of variations which are astonishingly vigorous and mature. One striking feature is the manual dexterity which they call into

[1] The exact date is not known. This collection with others has been printed by Dr. Fuller Maitland and Mr. W. B. Squire.

requisition. We are told that in the eighteenth
century the wife of Dr. Pepusch, a skilled player,
attempted to learn some of the pieces in the Fitzwilliam book, and had to retire baffled from the
first of them, John Bull's variations on Walsingham.
And if it be true, as is commonly asserted, that the
virginal technique of the time dispensed with both
thumb and little finger save at the extreme ends of
the phrase, we may accord to her our sincerest
sympathy. Many virtuosos of the present day
would think twice before essaying any of the
virginal books under those restrictions. But the
qualities which have made these collections a permanent possession are not those of skill and dexterity. Dürer sent his drawings to Raphael "to show
his hand," but he well knew how much head and
heart counted in their achievement. The brilliance
of our virginal writers and the learning of our
contrapuntists are alike the garments by which we
see the presence of an indwelling spirit.

CHAPTER IV

THE SEVENTEENTH CENTURY

GIBBONS is usually classed with the Elizabethan composers, and so far as concerns his madrigals this is in substance correct. It is true that he published them all after the Queen's death: the same may be said of some half-dozen among his contemporaries: East, for example, and Bateson, and Pilkington, and Thomas Tomkins, whose volumes appeared at intervals from 1604 to as late as 1622. In the annals of art and literature we seem to have adopted, for three centuries, an anti-Salic law under which succession followed the female line. Our three most famous periods are the Elizabethan, the Annian, and the Victorian. The latest of these extends to the verge of the Great War: our typical Annian poet is Pope, who produced the major part of his work in the reign of George II: it is appropriate that the madrigalian school which was one of the chief glories of Elizabeth's reign should hold until its close the title which she bequeathed to it. But though in his secular writings Gibbons is sealed of the tribe of Byrd and Wilbye, yet even here may be noted one stage of formal development. We have seen that the end of our sixteenth century was marked by a gradual emergence of scale from mode, bringing with it a fuller freedom of drawing and a wider range of harmonic colour. This change, which was tentative and experimental in Weelkes, became with Gibbons virtually complete. Thenceforward the modes pass rapidly out of use and are superseded by our own familiar system of major and minor, of diatonic and chromatic: it is not until our own day that the old vocabulary has been in part restored, and that largely as an antiquarian revival.

And if in his secular writing Gibbons plants his foot upon the frontier, in his Church music he definitely crosses it. The reforms in Italy which gave us opera and oratorio came to a head about 1600 and profoundly influenced the style of composition throughout Western Europe. It is no doubt a wild exaggeration to say that they "created monodic music" or "superseded polyphony"—the latter is not yet superseded and the former is as old as mankind—but they shifted the centre of gravity and brought into a new prominence some aspects of the musical art which had hitherto lain in the background. It is interesting that the earliest traces of the *Nuove Musiche* in England should so often appear among compositions for the Church. We may find them in the psalms of Michael East, with their quasi-dramatic style and their orchestral accompaniments: we may find them in Ward's anthem, "Let God arise," which almost anticipates the methods of the Restoration. Finest among all these are the services and anthems which, as organist of the Chapel Royal, Gibbons wrote from his appointment in 1604 to his death in 1625. Of his forty known anthems no less than twenty-five alternate chorus and "verse" or solo numbers, usually with independent accompaniment for strings or organ, and these include such masterpieces as "O all true faithful hearts" (a thanksgiving for the King's recovery from illness) and "This is the record of John," with its fine declamatory opening. He was no doubt a leader of both companies—we have but to recall such models of polyphonic writing as "Hosanna," "O clap your hands," and "Almighty and everlasting God"—in the extension and diffusion of new principles he was not only a leader but a pioneer.

We have said that Italian reformers gave us both opera and oratorio. In their early days the two forms were not very clearly distinguished: oratorio, which took its name from St. Philip Neri's church in Rome, soon transferred itself to the theatre when it found the most available place of public display and, perhaps for this reason, was of slow and retarded growth in England. Even Purcell never wrote oratorios: the form remained here in abeyance until it was introduced and popularized by Handel. The progress of the new music in this country is therefore chiefly to be exemplified by the chequered career of opera.

Dryden tells us that the first English opera was *The Siege of Rhodes*, by Sir William Davenant, which appeared with a somewhat apologetic manifesto in 1656. The way, however, had long been prepared not only by the incidental music of stage-plays, but still more by the masques which began to be organized about the turn of the century, and rose into high favour under our first two Stuart kings. These

were courtly entertainments,[1] given usually at
Whitehall or in some nobleman's house, and performed as a rule by amateurs of quality. They were
not, perhaps, strictly dramatic, for they had little
plot or action, but they brought into profuse combination poetry and music, song and dance, scenery
and pageant, gorgeous costumes and decorations;
and in this way opened a door through which the
whole forces of opera might readily enter. To them
some of the most renowned artists of the time
contributed: among their poets were Jonson and
Fletcher and Milton, among their composers
Lanière and Campian and Lock and Henry Lawes;
Inigo Jones designed the machinery and the costumes, Ferrabosco led the violins and controlled the
orchestra. The scale of outlay was lavishly sumptuous: the masque which celebrated the wedding of
Princess Elizabeth cost over £1000, and there were
many others in proportion. At least there was built
a rich palace for the dramatic spirit to inhabit: and
if we appraise dispassionately the dramatic value of
most operas we shall be less inclined to regret that
these early displays were satisfied with pageantry.

Of the music we have only tantalizing glimpses.
Many of the examples have perished, or remain
fragmentary and imperfect: in but a few instances
have we both melody and description, both text and
commentary. There are some charming songs by
Campian[2]; we are told that, in setting one of

[1] For the influence of Court pageants in Italian operatic history
see *L'Opéra avant l'opéra*, by Romain Rolland, and Heseltine's
monograph on Gesualdo, especially in reference to Ferrara.

[2] One is quoted by Sir Hubert Parry, *Oxford History of Music*,
vol. iii, p. 201.

Jonson's masques (1617), Nicholas Lanière introduced "the new art of recitativo," which was at first
received with some conservative misgivings; we
have more solid testimony in the music which Lawes
wrote for *Comus* and Lock for *Cupid and Death*, but
for the most part our evidence in this matter is slight
or indirect, gathered from a handful of surviving
examples or inferred from the recorded opinion of
the time.

There are three composers, in addition to those
already described, who demand here more than a
passing reference—Robert Johnson, Henry Lawes,
and Mathew Lock. Johnson (*d.* about 1634) was a
lutenist of such eminence that his name was in
public estimation coupled with that of Dowland.
He wrote in many forms—Church music, solo songs,
instrumental pieces—but it is in his work for the
stage that he is here chiefly memorable. He colla-
borated with Middleton in *The Witch*, with Beaumont and Fletcher in *Valentinian*, and with Ben
Jonson in *The Masque of Gypsies*: he was one of the
composers appointed for the opening of the New
Amphitheatre in 1611; his settings of "Where the
bee sucks" and "Full fathom five" are said to have
been those used at the opening performances of
The Tempest. His place among such a company is
sufficient evidence of his reputation in England: he
is one of the few English musicians whose name
was commemorated by the scholars and historians of
the Continent.[1] Henry Lawes (1595-1662) was
equally "fortunate in his alliances." In lyric song he
joined hands with Herrick and Waller, in masques

[1] See Parry, *Oxford History of Music*, vol. iii, pp. 75-76.

with Carey and Cartwright and Davenant: the height
of his fame was reached by the incidental music to
Comus (1634), which Milton requited with so royal
an encomium. He is the "Harry"

> Whose tuneful and well-measured song
> First taught our English music how to span
> Words with just note and accent

and who is placed for all time beside Dante's
Casella. It is true that some later critics, like
Burney and Hawkins, have found his melody
"insipid" and have complained that it is "neither
recitative nor air but so precise a medium between
both that a name is wanting for it": this is but the
obverse of Milton's praise, and the vocabulary of
music has discovered a name without difficulty. It
is true that Milton unduly depreciates the work of
other composers: that is but a friend's partiality
throwing into high relief a quality which is in itself
rightly estimated. At any rate from his judgment
there is no appeal. To be enshrined in that sonnet
is "like having your name written upon the dome
of St. Paul's": it shares the immortality of the monument which it adorns.

Last in order comes Matthew Lock (1630-1677),
Church composer, dramatic composer, and fighting
pamphleteer. He was brought up at Exeter in the
cathedral traditions: all that we know of his early
life is that he travelled in Flanders, collecting music
as he went: by 1653 he was established in London
where he wrote with Christopher Gibbons the songs
for Shirley's *Cupid and Death*. Three years later he

shared with Henry Lawes, Coleman, Cooke, and Hudson the music for Davenant's *Siege of Rhodes*, and at once rose to such reputation that Charles II, on his accession, appointed him "Master in the King's private music." He was only thirty at the time, and the jealousies which his elevation aroused were further embittered by his arrogance and ill-temper. Indeed a great part of his official life was taken up by acrimonious controversy on almost every subject, theoretical or practical, which came within the scope of his art. During the next ten years he composed but little: in the early 'seventies he made amends by producing the three master-pieces with which his name is chiefly associated, and which are landmarks in our operatic history. The first of these was to Davenant's adaptation of *Macbeth*, which appeared in 1672 and is of such quality that some critics, regardless of external evidence, have attributed it to Purcell.[1] Next year (1673-4) followed the instrumental music to Shad-well's *Tempest*, containing the famous "curtain tune,"[2] and the opera of *Psyche* (the words also by Shadwell) in which the style and manner of the masque are clearly merging into the more dramatic form that succeeded it. These two were published together in 1675 with a vehement manifesto on the principles of stage-music, and it is noticeable that after 1675 the masque fell into desuetude: its place taken in public display by the opera and in private

[1] Purcell was not yet fourteen years old. Even Mozart was twenty-four when he wrote *Idomeneo*.

[2] For an account of this see Parry, *Oxford History of Music*, vol. iii, pp. 75-76.

entertainment by its degenerate descendant, the
masquerade.

We have seen that the "first English opera"
presented itself in some disguise and was armed with
an apologetic plea for acceptance. The reason for
this was the prohibition of stage plays which was
passed by the Long Parliament and continued at
any rate officially, in force until the close of the
Commonwealth. Some impatient historians have
inferred that the Puritans were hostile to all forms
of recreation—to music among the rest: and this is
so grave a travesty of the facts that it deserves to be
considered in detail.

There were two forms of music to which the
Puritans objected—elaborate music in churches and
music of any kind in theatres. To the latter their
opposition was wholly uncompromising; they
detested the theatre as heartily as Tertullian himself,
and if we recall the post-Shakespearean theatre with
its "unfair subjects" we may feel that if we cannot
sympathize we can at any rate comprehend. To the
elaboration of Church music, and especially to the
organ accompaniment, they took exception partly
because it obscured the words, partly because Laud
approved of it, and chiefly because it recalled to
their minds the methods and usages of Rome. But
apart from an outbreak of fanatic zeal they seem to
have behaved with moderation. It is true that a law
of 1645 abolished the building of church organs.
It is true that in the early part of the Civil War there
were some deplorable incidents—we read, for
example, of a Roundhead army which captured
Exeter, dismantled the cathedral organ, and marched

through the streets blowing the pipes like flageolets. But against these may be quoted the instances in which organs were left undisturbed; in collegiate chapels such as St. John's, Oxford, and Christ's College, Cambridge, in the Cathedrals of St. Paul's, York, Durham, and Lincoln. It will be seen that even in this field the disaster was not so over-whelming as is commonly supposed.

And in regions remote from civic strife the art found large and peaceful habitations. Cromwell, who loved it, had a private organ of his own: so had Milton, who wrote about it with unfailing knowledge and devotion; Prynne, the fierce author of *Histriomastix*, approves it as "lawfull usefull and commendable"; Bunyan, who made a flute out of the leg of his prison chair, fills the dining-room of the House Beautiful with a concert of viols and virginals; the *Areopagitica*, written in the midst of the war, speaks of the "lutes, violins and ghitarrs in every house" and pleads for their freedom. And if further testimony is needed we may add that in this period of gloom and repression over thirty separate collections of music were published, including dances, catches, airs, dialogues and, what is more remarkable, the great corpus of polyphonic Eliza-bethan Church music edited by Barnard.

It is said that Cromwell inaugurated—he at any rate encouraged—the practice of public concerts at which audiences assembled to hear the performances of skilled musicians. This is so much a part of our customary life that we wonder at the idea of its ever having had a beginning: but no clear record of it can be found before the Commonwealth and it

was certainly in vogue then. His "master of music"
was John Hingston, who used to delight his leisure
with Latin motets, and had at command a great
number of virtuosi, both vocal and instrumental.
Playford, writing in 1651, enumerates some five
and twenty "cum multis aliis"; a catalogue which
would not shame the concert programmes of the
present generation. It is possibly a result of this
that the habit of amateur performances, so widely
prevalent in Elizabeth's time, began gradually to
die out. There were no doubt some enthusiastic
amateurs in the course of the century; Evelyn and
Roger North, Pepys with his preposterous "Beauty
retire," and Anthony à Wood with his Oxford
music meetings, "of which if I miss one I cannot
well enjoy myself the week after"; but as a general
rule this acceptance of music as a part of a gentleman's education declined under Charles II and concentrated executive skill into the hands of the professionals. Some morose critics attributed this to
the growing levity and frivolity of manners which
disinclined young people from taking trouble and
learning their gamuts: at any rate the change came
gradually about, and whereas a courtier of Elizabeth's reign would have felt shame if his musical
skill had been impugned, a courtier of Queen Anne
would have been almost insulted by the supposition
that he had any at all.

One general characteristic of English music in the
seventeenth century remains yet to be mentioned:
the vogue and excellence of our popular melodies,
both sacred and secular. Ravenscroft's *Pammelia* and
Deuteromelia were printed in 1609: his famous

Psalter followed in 1621 and was succeeded in its turn by Wither, Harper, Sandys, and many others: most famous of all was *The Dancing Master* of John Playford (himself also a capable editor of psalm tunes), which appeared in 1651 and ran through many editions. Our debt to Playford is almost incalculable. His collections and those which he inspired are fountain heads of national melody flowing as bright and sweet as on the day that they were written. Some are by known composers: Martin Parker (two of whose songs are sung by Maulkin in *The Compleat Angler*) contributed "When the King shall enjoy his own again" and "A country life is sweet"; Matthew Lock, "My lodging is on the cold ground"; William Lawes, "Gather ye rosebuds while ye may." Most are anonymous, like "Hunting the hare," "Love will find out the way," "The seeds of love," "The oak and the ash," and "The buff coat hath no fellow," which enjoyed a special popularity on the Restoration stage. Most of the songs written during the Commonwealth are, as might be expected, on the Cavalier side. One notable exception is the rollicking tune of "Hey, boys, up go we," which was adapted by the Roundheads to fit a manifesto against prelacy. But whatever their choice of party or their turn of sentiment they spring from a lively healthy love of music which gave the best of auguries for the advance of more serious composition.

So far we have traversed in this chapter a comparatively dull and low-lying stretch of country; a valley between the ranges of Elizabethan and Restoration music. We are now come to the further ascent and find, significantly enough, that our approach is by way of the Chapel Royal. In 1660 the Chapel, which had been disbanded for fourteen years, was reassembled and placed under the very competent direction of Captain Henry Cooke, an old Cavalier officer who had distinguished himself in the Civil War and who brought to his task not only a sound knowledge of music, but a keen sense of military discipline. He recruited his ranks by the methods of the pressgang, collected suitable boys from cathedrals and churches throughout the country, set them under an admirable system of education, and in a short time organized a choir which has never been surpassed in our musical history. Pepys, who disliked him and called him "a vain, conceited coxcomb," bears testimony to the excellence of the singing and the trained talent of the choristers: of the latter at least we may form our own judgment, for they included almost all the composers who rose to eminence during this period. Among the first boys to be admitted were Blow, Wise, Tudway, and Pelham Humfrey: Purcell followed in 1664; within a space of five years the whole leadership of Restoration music had assembled on this parade-ground.

First in date and first in promise was Pelham Humfrey, who was born in 1647. He was the most brilliant pupil of his time in the Chapel Royal: at the age of seventeen some of his anthems attracted the notice of Charles II who sent him to Paris in order that he might continue his education under Lully. Three years later he returned to England "a regular monsieur," as Pepys complains, and to his visit may be attributed in great measure the French influence which, under Royal encouragement, began to spread through our Restoration anthems and services. In 1672 he succeeded Captain Cooke as Master of the Choristers, in 1674 he died at the age of twenty-seven. In his grave, as in that of a greater musician than he, were buried "a rich possession and still fairer hopes."

His only known work for the stage consists of the vocal numbers and the masques which he contributed to Shadwell's version of *The Tempest* in 1674. Apart from this, a couple of ceremonial odes and a few songs, the whole of his writing was for the Church, and nearly all of it for the Chapel Royal. But he was essentially a dramatic composer in spirit. His anthems, notably "Rejoice in the Lord," "Have mercy upon me," "Hear, O Heavens," and "Like as the hart," show the influence of Lully and his theatre, not only in turns of melody but in the whole scheme and order of the construction. The solo voices often interplay in dialogue; the choruses join them in rapid alternations of response or commentary; the style is eloquent, declamatory, even oratorical, its chief aim not the pure dignity of worship but the full utterance of emotion. It has lost something in strength and opulence; it has gained in vividness of illustration.

Almost equal in promise, greater in achievement, was his fellow-chorister John Blow (1648-1708), whose sixty years of life were divided between his study and his organ-loft. He was twice organist of Westminster Abbey, the first time from 1668 to 1679, when he resigned in favour of his pupil Henry

Purcell, the second from 1695 when, on Purcell's death, he was reappointed to his old office. He was also Master of the Choristers at the Chapel Royal, and for a few years held a similar appointment at St. Paul's, besides being superintendent of music and later composer-in-ordinary to William III and Anne. Despite all this pressure of public work he was an abundant and prolific composer. In addition to some dozen ceremonial odes which the etiquette of the time demanded, he wrote 110 anthems and thirteen services, a considerable amount of virginal music, and many songs of which one collection, called *Amphion Anglicus*, was dedicated to Princess Anne and became widely popular. He was a master of bold and unexpected harmony; too adventurous indeed for the primness of our eighteenth-century criticism where Burney holds up his hands at "wanton violations of rule," and "licences which look and sound quite barbarous"[1]: but as usual time has brought its revenges and the rugged audacities have grown as sleek to our mouths as the names of Gordon and Macdonnell.[2] Indeed the examples with which Burney fills four protesting pages have been chosen by Sir Hubert Parry for special commendation. "For the most part," he says, "they do Dr. Blow great credit, for they show that he adventured beyond the mere conventional, and often with the success which betokens genuine musical insight."[3] And little deference to convention could be expected

[1] Burney, vol. iii, p. 448.
[2] See Milton's Sonnet on Tetrachordon, a valuable if indirect piece of musical criticism.
[3] *Oxford History of Music*, vol. iii, p. 275.

from an artist who, on receiving word from an exalted quarter that one of his anthems was too long, imperilled his office and his livelihood by replying, "That is the opinion of one fool. I heed it not." A very small proportion of his Church music is yet publicly accessible: but it is enough to assign him a high place in our musical history. He is not free from the mannerisms of his time—indeed he added some of his own—but his work whether vigorous or pathetic is always noble and in its most touching moments it drives straight to the heart. To our present generation he is best known by his songs, of which "The self-banished" (to name but one example) is a masterpiece of pure and expressive melody.[1]

The other two members of the group may be more summarily described. Tudway, organist of King's, Cambridge, and composer-in-ordinary to Queen Anne, was born in one of the later years of the Commonwealth and died in 1726. He was a musician of little originality whose own writings do not entitle him to consideration, but he deserves a place in our annals for the remarkable collection of cathedral music, in six volumes, which he compiled from 1714 to 1720 and which was the greatest monument of its kind since Barnard. In strong contrast is Michael Wise (1648-1687), almoner of St. Paul's Cathedral, who was killed in a street brawl at the age of thirty-nine: a ruffler of genius whose grave and dignified music matches oddly with what is known of his life and temper. Six of his anthems (including "Thy beauty, O Israel," and

[1] See Illustration H. i.

"Awake up my Glory," both of great merit) are published in Boyce's collection: others are contained in the choir-books of many cathedrals. Among all our Restoration composers he held most firmly to past tradition, and his best work catches at moments an afterglow and reflection of the Golden Age.

Such were the estuaries, in Swinburne's phrase, of that great sea which is Purcell: and it is on his name that this chapter can fittingly close. The facts of his life are hard to disentangle, partly from the imperfection of the record, partly from this conjecture of unthinking historians by whom obscurity has been further darkened.[1] One source of grave error has been the unwarranted assumption that when he supplied music for a play it was for the first performance, a conjecture which assigned his *Libertine* to 1676 and his *Epsom Wells* to 1672. Another, more serious because more misleading, has antedated his opera *Dido and Æneas* by some thirteen years, and has let loose a flood of admiring comment that so masterly and mature a work should have been produced by a boy of seventeen. We have enough evidence of his precocity without calling to our aid the miracles of an untenable legend.

He was born in 1659, the son of a musician who three years before had taken a part in Davenant's *Siege of Rhodes*. On his father's death in 1664 he was adopted by his uncle, Thomas Purcell, and entered at the Chapel Royal. We hear no more of him until 1670, when he set to music a loyal address from the

[1] Among the best accessible accounts are *Henry Purcell*, by Mr. Dennis Arundel, and the article by Barclay Squire and Colles in the third edition of Grove.

children on the occasion of His Majesty's birthday. This was his first known composition, and attracted so much attention that in 1673, when his voice broke and he had to leave the choir, he was at once appointed "keeper, maker, mender, repayrer and tuner" of the King's wind instruments with a salary of £30 a year and an allowance for wardrobe. It is interesting to note that the head of his department was John Hingston, who, when we last left him, was singing Latin motets to Oliver Cromwell. Music which weathered so many religious storms in Tudor times was still able to hold a straight course even through the perils of political change.

It is probable that during these years he was taking private lessons from John Blow, who had recently succeeded to the organistship of Westminster Abbey. It was at any rate there that, at the age of seventeen, he received his next official post, that of musical copyist to the Dean and Chapter. The havoc wrought in Church music by the excesses of the Commonwealth had largely expended itself on the choir-books, and it was no light task to gather up the scattered pages and to collate and edit them for the restored liturgy. But to Purcell this work must have been entirely congenial: it gave him a thorough grounding in contrapuntal technique, it enabled him to saturate his mind in the great Tudor tradition, and it bore fruit later in that superb set of polyphonic anthems, "Hear my prayer," "O God of hosts," "O God, thou hast cast us out," and "Jehova quam multi," which are worthy of being garnered with the harvests of Byrd and Tallis.

In 1679 he succeeded Blow as chief organist, and it

looked as though the main course of his life was predetermined. But the next year came two events which opened before him a new and divergent path: he was made master of the King's violins and he received his first commission to write for the stage. Both these turned his eyes in the direction of secular music, both had immediate effect on his composition. To the former we owe a collection of "Fantazias" for strings, in several parts; the forerunners of the famous sonatas which have given him his rank in the history of chamber music. The latter opened the gateway into a region where he won his principal triumphs and where his reputation is most firmly established. His first essay in this form was the incidental music to Nat Lee's *Theodosius*, a gorgeous exhibition of pagan splendour and christian martyr- dom which afforded Mrs. Barry a display of out- raged innocence and set society weeping. Purcell's contribution consisted of a ritual scene and a few songs, not of serious account for he was treading warily, but so well accepted that he had another commission within the year, and by 1690, when he entered upon his great dramatic period, had in- creased the number to about a dozen.

Meantime he was much occupied with official duties, with anthems for the abbey, with ceremonial odes, which began in 1680 and of which he wrote as many as twenty-nine, and with all the various details incidental to his station. In 1685 he wrote a magni- ficent anthem, solos, eight-part chorus, and orches- tra, for the coronation of James II[1]: it is not known

---

[1] See an account of this work in Mr. Arundel's volume, pp. 39 seq.

whether he did the same for William III but he certainly took part in the service, where he incurred a heavy censure by smuggling unauthorized visitors into the organ-loft. During these same years he was further advancing the cause of instrumental music. His early "Fantazias" had been modelled on the old madrigalian style of Gibbons, "apt for viols or voices": the twelve sonatas, for two violins and a bass, which he wrote in 1683, broke definitely with the English tradition and taught our native string-players the methods and idiom of Italy.[1] It is interesting to compare them with the first volume of Corelli which was published at Rome in the same year. Corelli is the greater virtuoso, Purcell the greater composer; one shows a more intimate knowledge of the violin, the other a wider range of invention and a freer flexibility of design. Some years after (the exact date is uncertain) he added the ten "sonatas of four parts" which were published after his death and in which the finest of his instrumental music is contained. The ninth of these has become famous under its title of *The Golden Sonata*— it is close matched by the passacaglia of the sixth and the fugal canzonas of the fourth and seventh.

The success of *Dido and Æneas*, written in 1688 for a girls' school, determined still further the bent of Purcell's genius for the stage. In 1690 he produced *Dioclesian*, an adaptation of Beaumont and Fletcher's *Prophetess*, which so hit the taste of the town that in the next year he took the very unusual step of publishing the music. From that time to his death

[1] See the preface in which he avows his preference of Italian music to French.

in 1695 he wrote no less than forty-four dramatic works, many of them in collaboration with Dryden, and though his contribution was often restricted to a few songs or instrumental pieces, yet on occasion he took his full share and joined with the poet in equal partnership. *Dioclesian,* for instance, is on the large operatic scale: so is *King Arthur* (1691): so are *The Fairy Queen* (1692) and, as far as we know it, *The Tempest*[1] (? 1695). All these are described in contemporary records as "operas" and they well merit the title. They lead direct to the operas of Handel, before whose noonday splendour they rise as a fitting dawn.

Indeed, as is so often the case with short-lived composers, nearly all Purcell's most notable work was crowded into his last few years. *The Yorkshire Feast-song* is of the same year as *Dioclesian,* the ode, "Welcome, glorious morn," of the same year as *King Arthur,* the "Te Deum" and "Jubilate in D" celebrated the festival of St. Cecilia's Day in 1694, the anthem, "Thou knowest, Lord," was written for the funeral of Queen Mary in 1695. His last work "written by Mr. Purcell in his sickness" was the song, "From rosie bowers," intended for the third part of d'Urfey's *Don Quixote,* an opera which he did not live to complete. Many of his songs were collected and published after his death under the title of *Orpheus Britannicus*: other posthumous publications were the "Te Deum" and "Jubilate," the Harpsichord lessons, a collection of *Ayres for the Theatre,* and the second set of sonatas.

[1] The whole bibliography of *The Tempest* is still under investigation.

There is probably no great composer whose work it is more difficult to appraise. As M. Rolland says, "it rests incomplete," rising at some moments to the highest summit of genius, sinking at others to an almost perfunctory commonplace. It has been suggested that one reason for his inequality is his profusion. In a short life crowded with official duties he wrote over seventy anthems, over fifty operas and dramatic pieces, nearly thirty odes and over two hundred songs, besides a large quantity of instrumental music: yet it is hard to maintain the plea if we look at the Bachgesellschaft edition or recall the boundless abundance of Mozart and Schubert. It is better to illustrate the fact than to form any curious researches into its cause, and though the bare mention of his shortcomings is irksome and distasteful it may throw his transcendent merits into brighter relief.

There are, then, three principal respects in which, as it seems to me, he has given hostages to fortune. The first is that his melody is not always, nor very often, of the supremely highest rank. It is pure, it is lucid, it is imbued with national feeling, but it does not worship in the inner courts. As Mallarmé said of the Parnassians, "*ça manque de mystère.*" I would offer as example two well-known songs of which one seems to me to attain and the other to miss the note of perfection. The song, "I attempt from Love's sickness to fly," seems to me one of the most beautiful in the world;[1] not Mozart nor

---

[1] See Illustration H. ii. I venture to disagree with those critics who have found in this song traces of Lully's influence. It seems to me pure Purcell at his best.

Schubert have more delight of melody or more firmness of construction. The song, "Nymphs and Shepherds," which is often associated with it, seems to me on an entirely different level: it is clear and tuneful and well adapted to the voice but the most intimate secrets of music are closed to it. And I find among Purcell's melodies more examples of the latter sort than of the former. Even "Fairest Isle" is nearer akin to "Rule Britannia" than to "God preserve the Emperor."

The second is that no artist of his eminence has ever been so completely under the control of one tiresome mannerism. On almost every occasion when joy or praise or jubilation is indicated, on almost every occasion when the music speaks with a cheerful voice, we have the same lilting figure of dotted notes constantly appearing until we come to expect it as a matter of course. It is of no use for his apologists to say that his music "contains but a single cliché" when we can hardly open an ode or an anthem without finding it. Not Mendelssohn with his unfailing cadence or Chopin with his persistent formula is so much at the mercy of his own creation. No doubt it springs from a naïve pleasure in a new device of expression, but Purcell would surely have been well advised if he had followed the counsel of one of his own soloists and let his moderation be known unto all men.

The third is one which he shares with other composers of the seventeenth and eighteenth centuries. Every age has its conventions; one which belonged especially to that period was the construction of a song on a single quatrain, or an even more

slender foundation, the words of which were
constantly repeated in order to eke out the music.
Handel is a conspicuous example of this parsimony,
but his closest economies are generous beside some
of Purcell's. In one song a stanza ends with the artless couplet:

> No joys are above
> The pleasures of love,

which appears in *Orpheus Britannicus* as

> "No, no, no, no joys are above the pleasures
> of love, no joys are above the pleasures of love,
> no, no, no, no, no, no, no, no joys are above,
> no, no, no, no, no, no, no joys are above the
> pleasures of love the pleasures of love."

Another in more meditative tone contains the
dignified panegyric:

> None were more ready in distress to save;
> None were more loyal, none more brave,

which loses all its dignity and most of its significance when it is expanded into the form:

> "None were more ready, none were more
> ready, none, none, none none, none were more
> ready in distress to save; none, none, none, none,
> none, none, none, none, none were more loyal
> none more brave."

This is really worse than the trailing syllables of our
mediæval composers, and though it seems to have

excited no comment at the time, we may find in it
a reason why some of Purcell's finest music has not
yet returned to our concert-room.

Ad lætiora vertamus. These defects, even if they
have been fairly stated, are as nothing, beside the
splendour of his invention, the depth of his feeling,
and the mastery with which he governs every
musical form known in his time. His Church music
combines the strength and solidity of the Elizabethan period with the warmth and colour of the new
harmony: we have but to recall such examples as
"Hear my prayer," "Jehovah quam multi" (especially the section "Ego cubui et dormivi"), and
"My heart is inditing" to see in full flight the ascent
which soared at last into the "Te Deum" and "Jubilate" of his later years.[1] His declamation is un-
usually just, his pathos true and poignant, on
occasion, as in the stilling of the storm from "They
that go down," he can paint a scene in a few strokes
which set it before us as a possession for ever. His
gift of vivid and picturesque presentation finds full
scope in his music for the theatre. *Dido and Æneas*, for
example, shows a power of characterization such as
the world did not see again until the time of Gluck.
King Arthur, "negligible as a play," is transfigured
by its musical setting: *The Fairy Queen* (a wild
adaptation of Shakespeare's *Midsummer Night*), is a
pageant of rich tunes and delightful textures. The
veriest hint of a scene or a situation was enough to
catch his fancy, the rococo structures glowed and
mellowed in the light of his genius.

The odes and welcome-songs were ceremonial

[1] See Illustration I.

pieces, written at command and as full of pious
flattery as an Augustan poet. They bore, however,
no other resemblance to Horace and Virgil: the
words were poor and illiterate, and Purcell's only
course was to disregard them in detail and paint
with a broad brush. But the music is often at a high
level. There is a wonderful feeling for atmosphere
in the tenor solo of the *Yorkshire Feast-Song*; the
hymn, "Soul of the world," from the Cecilia Ode
of 1692, is in Purcell's most exalted manner, the
royal numbers have often an exhilarating sense of
pageantry like the drums and trumpets at a military
parade. On the whole these works are the most
unequal that he composed; at their best they attain
heights which even he never overtopped.

A special word should be said on Purcell's
treatment of the musical device called a ground bass:
a recurrent staple of melody on which the other
parts are woven in the form of variations. In
unskilled hands it has often become dull and
monotonous: in such numbers, as Handel's "Envy"
chorus, Bach's Passacaglia, and the finale of Brahms'
Fourth Symphony it is extraordinarily effective for
close-knit texture and ingenious surprises of
harmony. Of this form Purcell had a remarkable
control. Two examples, well known to all who have
followed his work, are the "Lament" in *Dido and
Æneas*, and the still more beautiful setting of Ken's
"Evening Hymn," with its close of chanting
Alleluias. They are of the great company, and there
are many others of almost equal rank.

In a summary such as this it would be impossible
to enumerate all the salient features of his writing:

they can now be studied at leisure in the scholarly volumes of the Purcell Society. It is enough to say that after nearly two centuries of neglect he has come to his own and that his worth can be attested not by second-hand rumours but by close and appreciative understanding. He is not, perhaps, "England's greatest composer": if that place be assigned to any one (and such comparisons are usually tedious), it is held as of right by William Byrd. But among all the composers of our great period he is the one who stands nearest to us—whose voice and accent are most familiar in our ears. Had he lived to found a school we might have continued to rival in unbroken succession the music of the continental nations. Fate which robbed us of this has set him at the close of a dynasty and has raised to him for all time an imperishable monument.

CHAPTER V

THE DARK AGE

THE course of English music in the eighteenth century was seriously impeded by two obstacles. First of these was the growing concentration of all social life on London and its immediate neighbourhood. No doubt there were the watering-places—Bath and Buxton and Harrogate—but these were only transient pleasure-grounds, and it is noticeable that the most popular of them—Hampstead, Bagnigge Wells, Epsom, and Tunbridge—were all within easy reach of the capital. For country life and country pursuits Londoners, apart from a few sportsmen, had an unqualified contempt. They disliked its scenery—their favourite epithet for any mountainous region was "horrid"—they found its simplicity wearisome and its routine monotonous; to travel beyond Twickenham was to go into exile beset with dangers and discomforts for which there were no compensations. The testimony is constant and unanimous. "I hate," says a disconsolate Annian poet:

> I hate the brook that murmurs at my feet,
> Give me the kennels of St. James's Street:
> And, when on sultry days I pant for air,
> Give me the breezes of St. James's Square.

In Swift's Polite Conversation, an invaluable document for the manners of the mid-century, the Londoners, whose own repartees do not entitle them to any airs of superiority, fall with one consent upon the luckless Derbyshire baronet whose presence they resent and whose rusticity they despise. And the greatest Englishman of the age clenches the whole matter in a single sentence: "When a man is tired of London he is tired of life: for there is in London all that life can afford."[1]

The second obstacle, part symptom and part cause, was the almost formal exclusion of music from a liberal education. No longer were the part-books "set out after supper": their places were taken by the card-table and the punch-bowl. No longer was the lute "as familiar to a gentleman as his sword": the strings were frozen into silence amid an atmosphere of apathy or disdain. Music, which had once been a native art sank to the level of a fashionable entertainment in which foreign composers gave opportunities of display to foreign virtuosi, and an uncomprehending public received the performance with alternations of total disregard and misplaced enthusiasm. A popular singer like Farinelli could pay off the debt on Lincoln's Inn Fields, and then erect out of the balance a "very superb mansion," which he called by the appropriate name of England's Folly: we may estimate the artistic value of his success when we are told that he was once applauded for over five minutes on singing the first note of an operatic song. Both in what it gave and in what it withheld, our Augustan age sank to the lowest

[1] Boswell's *Johnson*, s.v., 1777.

nadir that has ever been touched by English music.

As might be expected, the tendencies of the time are accentuated in its literary history. Among our great Annian writers there is not one, except Arbuthnot, who shows the slightest sympathy with music or the slightest understanding of its influence. Swift hated it, Pope hated it, Addison pierced it with shafts of gentle irony, Steele bent a less efficient bow on the side of Addison: the chief musical controversy of the time was dismissed as an affair of Tweedledum and Tweedledee. It is indeed intelligible on other grounds that music and letters should have suffered a temporary estrangement. The whole temper of the time was political: it was a golden age of satirists and pamphleteers: successful men of letters were those who, like Swift and Addison, could be enlisted in the ranks of controversy, or who like Pope could win their way by argument and epigram. There was little room for the higher flights of imagination, or for that pure and mystic insight in which music and poetry approach most nearly to each other. It is true that Pope wrote an Ode on St. Cecilia, and Addison an opera-libretto. The former, composed "invitissima Minerva," is a frigid production marked by an entire absence of lyrical gift, the latter is an unaccountable excursion into wholly unfamiliar territory where both author and musician incurred equal disaster. Music could hope for little co-operation from a sister art whose sublimest utterances were Swift's poem on the Day of Judgment and the peroration of *The Dunciad*.

Purcell, as we have seen, left no school. Of the

composers who follow him most closely in point of
time the most notable are Clarke and Croft, and
neither of these approaches the first rank, though
Croft's name is still celebrated by the stately music
which he wrote for our funeral service. One verse
of this is incorporated from Purcell, for whom Croft
in his preface expresses a warm regard and affection.
It is the last vestige of Astræa before she leaves a
land that has become unworthy of her presence.

At the end of 1710 Handel paid his first visit to
London. It was a voyage of adventure, for he had
no acquaintance in our country and knew no word
of our language, but he bore with him a double
reputation—that of his triumphal progress through
Italy and that of his recent appointment as Kapell-
meister to the elector of Hanover. On his arrival he
was introduced to Aaron Hill, manager of the
Haymarket theatre, who offered him a libretto based
on an episode in Tasso's *Jerusalem*—the same that
was afterwards used by Gluck for his *Armida*.
Handel wrote the music in a fortnight; a first-rate
company of Italian singers was engaged: on 24th
February 1711 *Rinaldo* was produced on a scale of
unprecedented magnificence and at once took the
town by storm. Addison in the fifth number of
the *Spectator* ridiculed the artificial language and the
elaboration of the stage appliances; but before the
music criticism was silent, and the populace, which
was chiefly interested in the scenery, crowded the
playhouse for no less than fifteen representations.
It is not fair to say that *Rinaldo* killed English music:
there was then no English music to kill; our chief
representatives were the "Swiss Count" Heidegger,

who managed the opera at the Queen's Theatre, and Dr. Pepusch of Berlin, who was organist to the Duke of Chandos. But we cannot claim it as in any sense our own: to its irresistible invasion we contributed only the conquered territory.

For six months Handel remained in London, fêted, caressed, encouraged by wealthy patrons, and paying his tribute to native art by attending the concerts of "Thomas Britton, the musical small-coal man." The next five years he divided between this country and Hanover, and his principal works were the Utrecht "Te Deum," for which Queen Anne gave him a pension, the opera of *Teseo*, perhaps the Water Music, and the setting of Brockes' "Passion," which was his last composition to a German text. In 1717 he succeeded Pepusch as organist to the Duke of Chandos and from thenceforward made England his home. Nine years later he was naturalized as a British subject.

The first-fruits of his permanent residence in England were the "Chandos Anthems," the pastoral *Acis and Galatea*, and the oratorio of *Esther*. But memories of *Rinaldo* and *Teseo* turned his mind towards opera, and to this he devoted the greater part of his energy and genius for the next two and twenty years. At first the omens were favourable. George I gave the scheme his patronage, a guarantee fund of £50,000 was collected, the Haymarket theatre was remodelled under the title of the Royal Academy of Music, Handel, Bononcini, and Ariosti assumed the joint direction, and among the singers were Durastanti, the prima donna, Broschi the most famous bass in Europe, and for climax of splendour Francesco Senesino. Then followed a period of ceaseless conflict. Bononcini proved to be an unscrupulous intriguer with whom no co-operation was possible; Cuzzoni, engaged for the third season, was a spitfire whom Handel had to subdue with threats of personal violence; Faustina, her principal rival, was worse than Cuzzoni: as climax of misfortune the Prince of Wales quarrelled with his father and carried off a large following of seceders to the opposition theatre in Lincoln's Inn Fields. Amid all this turmoil Handel held a distracted course. During the next ten years he wrote a dozen important works for the stage, including *Giulio Cesare* and *Tameriano*, both of which largely increased the scope of dramatic music, and the former of which contains, in addition, some notable experiments in orchestral colour. The public, however, cared nothing for structure or orchestration; all that it wanted was to be presented with amusing novelties: as it grew familiar with these pageantries, so it became weary of them, and not even Handel's melody could retain its interest. The crisis came in 1728 when he was swept into bankruptcy by the rise of a new favourite.

This was the *Beggar's Opera*, "an odd, pretty sort of thing," for which Gay wrote the words and Pepusch compiled the music. It was produced at Lincoln's Inn Fields and had a wide and immediate success; it ran for sixty-two nights in London, it spread like wildfire through the fashionable watering-places, it was in Paris by the middle of the century and in America before the end. It had indeed many claims to popular regard. It was written by a celebrated man of letters, it was whimsical and tuneful, above all it was held to be a political satire and to contain a most telling attack upon Sir Robert Walpole and the King's party. That it should have entertained the town is no matter for surprise; the wonder is that an antagonist so lightly equipped should have inflicted so overwhelming a defeat.

Handel took the disaster philosophically, engaged fresh singers, went into partnership with Heidegger, and set himself to rebuild from the ground his fallen fortunes. But the public, constant only to inconstancy, had largely deserted him. One by one his singers transferred their allegiance: in 1734 he gave up the Haymarket and moved into less expensive quarters: in 1737 he was bankrupt for the second time and his career as opera-manager was at an end. He had written forty dramatic works of immeasurably higher quality than those against which he contended. When, a few years later, Gluck was seeking consolation for his failure in London, Handel supplied it from his own experience. "The reason is simple," he said, "you have taken too much trouble for the English."

He was now fifty-two years of age. In a quarter of a century he had passed through every vicissitude of fortune: in 1711 he was "the Orpheus of our age," in 1737 he was a broken and ruined man, faced with the necessity of meeting his creditors and threatened with paralysis. But his courage and resource were indomitable. He went to Aix and restored his health: he gave a benefit concert on his return, and paid off his debts: he reviewed his position and with all the confidence of youth set out on a new adventure—the conquest of oratorio. He had already made three tentative essays in this form: *Esther* (1717), *Deborah*, and *Athaliah* (1733). He now took it in hand to fuller purpose and expended on it the chief remaining energies of his life. *Saul* and *Israel* appeared in 1738-9: next year followed *L'Allegro, Il Penseroso ed Il Moderato*, in the words of which Milton joined hands with the Rev. Charles Jennens; and so the catalogue unfolds—twenty-five works in all—until the production of his last composition, *Jephtha*, at the beginning of 1752. They were by no means uniformly successful. *Samson* was well received, so was *Judas Maccabæus*, which was written to commemorate the victory at Culloden, so apparently were *Semele* and *Jephtha*; the rest were often treated with disregard or interrupted by the more vivacious members of the opposition party. *Israel*, for example, was a failure: *Theodora*, in spite of "Angels ever bright and fair," was played to empty benches ("you could have danced there," was Handel's indignant comment): most remarkable of all, *The Messiah*, which was produced and acclaimed in Dublin, was on its return to London heard with stolid indifference. It was put on after the successful run of *Samson*, and in spite of the King's presence, fell so flat that it had to be withdrawn after two performances. Not until seven years later did it acquire the favour of the English public. Horace Walpole sums up the popular verdict in a letter to Sir Horace Mann (24th February 1743):

"Handel has set up an Oratorio against the

Opera and succeeds. He has hired all the god-
desses from farces and all the singers of Roast
Beef from between the acts of both theatres, with
a man with one note in his voice and a girl with
never an one, and so they sing and make brave
Hallelujahs."

In 1745 he was attacked by illness and driven into
his third bankruptcy, but neither misfortune could
dim his genius or his courage, and to his last active
years belong such masterpieces as *Semele, Joshua,
Theodora, Solomon,* and *Jephtha.* In 1752 he under-
went three operations for *gutta serena,* and in 1753
he became totally blind. He died in 1759.

On his death there was a revulsion of feeling: the
children of those who had stoned the prophet were
assiduous in building his sepulchre. The centenary
festival of 1784, held in Westminster Abbey, was a
worthy, if sorely belated, monument to his name:
it was repeated four times in the next seven years:
and it is not too much to say that from thenceforward to the present generation he dominated the
course of music in this country. *The Messiah* has
been more often performed here than any other
existing composition; it is still the mainstay of our
three-choir festivals and the recurrent delight of our
northern choral societies. And if we are seldom
adventurous enough to explore further,[1] it is at
least something that we have taken home to our

---

[1] The Handel Festival held triennially at the Crystal Palace has
traditionally occupied three days: the first given to *The Messiah,*
the last to *The Israel,* and the intervening day to a smaller work
and a miscellaneous selection.

H   E.M.

business and bosoms one work, and that of supreme value, which he has left us as an inheritance.

This is not the place to describe in any detail the measure of Handel's astonishing gifts: the fertility of invention which never fails, the command of technical resources which makes every problem look easy, the Alpine sublimity of his choral writing, the range and intimacy of his expression: above all, the sheer delight of melody which for intrinsic loveliness has never been surpassed. The composer who was a chosen hero to Mozart, to Beethoven, to Schubert, and to Brahms is in no need of our encomium and can afford to smile at our criticism. But we have no part or lot in him. We welcomed him at first as an exotic novelty, we gave him from time to time a little intermittent and capricious patronage, but we rejected some of his best work; we ruined him three times, we allowed his whole life to be embittered with constant intrigue and controversy. When we assemble at the present day for the enjoyment of his chief masterpiece we had better come in sackcloth and ashes.

Of the Church composers who followed after Croft the highest in contemporary estimate was Maurice Greene—the "Dr. Blue" of Arbuthnot's satire. He was born in 1695, educated at St. Paul's, trod the usual round of official posts and ultimately succeeded Croft as organist of the Chapel Royal and Tudway as Professor of Music at Cambridge. In his early years he was a close personal friend of Handel, who used frequently to extemporize on his organ, but when the great quarrel came he sided with Bononcini, and the breach was too wide to be healed. Much of his work remains in manuscript, his chief publication was the volume of *Forty Select Anthems*, which he printed in 1743. These do not often rise above mediocrity—they are cast in an inferior metal from the designs of Blow and Purcell —but exception must be made in favour of the pathetic "Lord, how long wilt thou be angry," and the funeral march-movement of "Lord, let me know mine end." He did better service to his art when he employed the leisure of his later years on a collection of English cathedral music which he bequeathed for completion to his pupil William Boyce.

Of different quality was Thomas Augustine Arne (1710-1789), the son of a London tradesman who is said to have been the model for Addison's "Political Upholsterer." He was educated at Eton and intended for the Law, but his bent for music was too strong to be resisted and after a few fruitless struggles his father gave way and allowed him to indulge his genius. His first essays as a composer were incidental pieces for the Haymarket: in 1738 he made his reputation by setting an adapted version of *Comus*; in 1740 he enhanced it with the masque of *Alfred*, which contains "Rule Britannia," and the songs to *As you Like it*, two of which, "When daisies pied" and "Blow, blow, thou winter wind," still retain a place in our affections. The next few years were mainly spent in Dublin where, with his wife, a celebrated bravura singer, he won great success, and where he produced his operatic oratorio of *Abel*. The last oratorio which had been produced in Dublin was *The Messiah*.

By 1745 he was back in London, where he wrote

Colin and Phœbe for Vauxhall Gardens and the incidental music to *The Tempest* on its revival at Drury Lane. The song, "Where the bee sucks," which breathes the very spirit of Ariel, was written for this occasion. Of the next ten years there is little or no record; he was probably occupied in supplying varied entertainments for the gardens of Ranelagh, Vauxhall, and Marylebone. In 1759 he received the Doctorate of Music at Oxford: a generous academic recognition of one whose work had wandered so far from academic lines, and it was perhaps the incitement of this new-won honour that led him forthwith to abandon his accustomed manner and produce a full-dress tragic opera in the Italian style with every device of elaboration which the tradition and experience of the art could suggest. *Artaxerxes* was, indeed, too elaborate to be successful: it bewildered more than it pleased, and its tenure of life was distressingly short. But a few of the simpler songs outlasted the drums and tramplings, and one of them, "Water parted from the sea," well deserves the immortality which Goldsmith in *She Stoops to Conquer* has conferred upon it. Another grand opera—a setting of Metastasio's *Olympiade* with Italian text—was an even more disastrous failure, due, it is said, to those internal jealousies from which the playhouse was not often free. But a contributary cause is that suggested by Horace Walpole who, when Covent Garden was burned down, openly rejoiced on the ground that "the nation has long been tired of operas and has now a good opportunity of dropping them."

Of his other serious works a brief mention must

suffice. His oratorio, *Judith*, produced in 1761, is notable as the earliest composition of its kind which admitted female voices into the chorus: a daring innovation which not only altered its balance, but affected in no small degree its quality of tone. In 1769, despite a quarrel with Garrick, he wrote some of the music for the Shakespeare Jubilee at Stratford. Next year came a garbled version of Dryden's *King Arthur*, in proposing which he treats Purcell's melodies with great disparagement. Among his last compositions was a setting of Mason's *Caractacus*, which appeared shortly before his death, in 1775. Beside these he wrote a vast number of glees, catches, canons, and other *pieces d'occasion*, together with some twenty books of songs contributed by him to plays and other forms of popular entertainment.

Arne was the only English composer of this period to whom the title of genius can with any propriety be assigned. He carries light armour: he wins by readiness of attack and dexterity of movement: he is less at his ease in the larger and more stately exercises of art than in those of the pleasaunce and the playing ground: but his sentiment, if a little shallow, is always sincere and his melody is delightfully fresh and spontaneous. In an age when our music had become dull and academic he lightened it with a native wood-note of genuine sweetness and charm: and though he seldom rises to the first order, and that only for moments, he takes an honourable rank in the second.

An almost exact contemporary of Arne was Charles Avison (1710-1770), who is of some historical

interest, partly because his name has been revived by
Robert Browning, partly because he was deliberately
set up in the north of England as the rival and
antagonist of Handel. He was organist of St.
Nicholas, Newcastle, and a voluminous composer
of concertos and sonatas: some for full orchestra,
others for the unusual combination of harpsichord
and two violins. His principal work was the *Essay
on Musical Expression* (1752), in which he extolled
his old master, Geminiani, and depreciated Handel's
instrumental writing; but his treatise is now as
completely forgotten as the controversy to which
it gave rise, and we may justly dismiss him as a
person of some importance in his day.

Another contemporary of Arne was William
Boyce (1710-1779), a famous organist and chorus-
master, who rose to be composer to the Chapel
Royal and conductor of the three-choir festivals.
He wrote in almost all the current forms—masques,
serenatas, Church music, and when Master of the
King's band accomplished the incredible task of
setting forty-three adulatory odes by William
Whitehead, the poet-laureate. As a composer he is
chiefly known to us by a few anthems and by the
song "Heart of Oak"—a sound, forthright tune,
to words by Garrick which first appeared in an
extravaganza called *Harlequin's Invasion*. But his real
monument is the collection of English cathedral
music, in three volumes, which he inherited from his
old master, Maurice Greene, and carried a stage nearer
completion. It is not an impeccable work: both as
researcher and as editor he leaves something to be
desired: but it helped to keep alive many composi-

tions, especially of Gibbons, Blow, and Purcell, which might otherwise have sunk into oblivion.

Mention has been made of the three-choir festivals. These were started in 1724 at Gloucester, and were held in annual rotation by combining the musical societies of that city and those of Worcester and Hereford. At first they were simple and informal— two morning performances of liturgical music in the cathedral and one "entertainment" in the city hall, with an occasional virtuoso to enhance the local resources. From 1737, when Boyce was appointed conductor, they enlarged their scope and included oratorios and other important compositions by Boyce, Greene, and especially Handel. In 1759, the year of Handel's death, they gave *The Messiah* in Hereford Cathedral and so inaugurated a custom which has continued without intermission for over 170 years. Other similar festivals followed in due course: Birmingham in 1768, Norwich in 1770, Chester in 1772, and to these is largely due the growth of Handel's influence which permeated English musical life during the latter part of the eighteenth century and the first three-quarters of the nineteenth.

Among the musical events of the mid-century, one of the highest importance was the production and use of our National Anthem, which was first sung at Covent Garden on 28th September 1745 — the occasion of Sir John Cope's defeat at Prestonpans— and was printed by the *Gentleman's Magazine* in October of the same year. Its origin has been the subject of much controversy. It has been assigned to Henry Carey, because his son claimed it fifty-two years later as a pretext for a pension; it has been assigned on insufficient grounds to Lully; it has been claimed, on no grounds at all, for Germany;[1] it was used in Russia when Lvoff superseded it with his famous "Hymn to the Tsar." One theory alone remains, and although it is hedged about with difficulties it is, on our present evidence, the most probable.

The anthem was, as we have seen, first publicly sung in 1745. At that time one of the leaders of musical life in London was Dr. Pepusch, an enthusiastic collector of old English music, who is known to have had in his possession a manuscript volume of pieces for virginals and organ by the Elizabethan composer John Bull. Pepusch bequeathed this volume to his friend William Kitchener, at whose sale in 1827 it was bought by a gentleman of the Chapel Royal called Richard Clark. Clark was evidently much occupied with the attribution of "God Save the King," and published two dissertations on the subject. In the first (1814) he accepted Carey's claim, in the second (1822) he altered his mind and declared in favour of Bull. The volume contained an "ayre" in triple time which Clark put forward as the original of the melody: this he showed to Sir George Smart, who transcribed it, and the transcription is now extant and may be seen in Grove's *Dictionary*.[2]

---

[1] The "German National Anthem," "Heil dir im Siegerkranz," was written for Christian VII of Denmark in 1790, and announced as being set "to the melody of the English 'God save great George our King.'" See Grove, vol. ii, p. 602, which quotes the passage from the *Flensburger Wochenblatt* of 27th January 1790.

[2] Vol. ii, p. 407. See Illustration J.

From this tangle of evidence the following facts seem to emerge. First that the "ayre" transcribed by Sir George Smart bears, as it stands, so close a resemblance to "God Save the King" that the possibility of coincidence is entirely excluded. Secondly, that if the appropriate key signature be added, a feat of which any adapter is capable, the resemblance becomes a virtual identity. The two tunes are in the same stanza, a stanza so unusual that in the whole range of English music up to that time I have found no other example: of the fourteen bars which they respectively comprise the first six are substantially the same, the next four are *verbatim et literatim* the same: only in the last four is there a difference of phrase, and it is in these that the principal variant of the National Anthem occurs. What should we say if we were told that there were only two sonnets in the Petrarchian form and that ten out of their fourteen lines were to all intents and purposes identical?

Our difficulties, however, are not at an end. We are told that Clark tampered with the tune, and verification is here impossible for the manuscript has disappeared. It is certainly an unfortunate circumstance that he wrote his palinode in favour of John Bull five years before the manuscript came into his possession; but this is not insuperable, for he may well have seen it in Dr. Kitchener's famous library. It may well be that having formed his new opinion he "gave a cocked hat and sword" to the evidence in its favour: that would not be enough to account for the resemblance. For it is not a matter of detail that is at issue; not the alteration of a few notes in a curve; it is the whole foundation and structure of the melody. Nothing short of a complete forgery would be enough to sustain the charge, and this at any rate has never been alleged.

The conclusions to which we are led is that "God Save the King" is based on Dr. Bull's "Ayre,"[1] moulded and adapted by an eighteenth-century hand. We do not know, and shall probably never know, who its adaptor was. Carey's plea is not serious and there is no one else in the field. But at least we may claim it for our own nation, and carry back its origin to the spacious times of our musical pre-eminence.

The latter part of our eighteenth century was as undistinguished as the earlier. London was still the land of El Dorado to foreign musicians—Abel and J. C. Bach provided our fashionable concerts, Sacchini presided for some years over the opera, Muzio Clementi introduced us to the pianoforte, Giardini played our violin solos and led our orchestra. Among them were two far more august visitors: Mozart, who came as a child in 1764, and so astonished the connoisseurs that a paper on him was read before the Royal Society: Haydn, who came twice, in 1791 and 1794, and enriched us with the gift of his twelve Salomon symphonies. But all this opulence only brought into fuller relief the barrenness of our own land: at a time when the riches of symphony, sonata, and quartet were being garnered elsewhere we could only hold out our hands and contribute to them nothing.

[1] Dr. Fuller Maitland has traced a quotation from it to a catch of Purcell. See *O.H.M.*, vol. iv, 2nd edition, Preface, and p. 347.

Yet we were not without some evidence of musical activity. Our Church composers, Battishill, Arnold and Crotch, maintained with dignity the tradition of the English service; Samuel Wesley, who towers above them all is still remembered by such noble motets as "Exultate" and "In exitu Israel." Again there are two tiny forms which appeared about this time and which may be regarded as distinctively English in origin. One was the Glee, an unaccompanied vocal composition which differed from the Church part-song in being written for solo voices and from the madrigal in being not contrapuntal but harmonic in texture. It was centralized by the establishment of the Glee Club in 1783, and soon became widely popular. Its characteristic smoothness and sweetness made it easy to sing and pleasant to hear: for half a century and more it was a favourite resource of British composers. Chief among the glee writers was Samuel Webbe, whose "Glorious Apollo" is still historical. Among the others were Attwood, Battishill, Cooke, Lord Mornington, and Spofforth, whose ingenious toys, though of no great or permanent value, served to fill many agreeable hours of leisure. The other "English" form was the Ballad Opera, a slender comedy usually rustic in character, with spoken dialogue and simple songs and ensembles. Its pioneer was Arne's *Love in a Village* (1762), which gives it some slight priority over Hiller's *Singspiele*, as well as over the *Opéra Comique* of France and the *Zarzuela* of Spain: at any rate it seems to have started on its own course without any indebtedness to its continental neighbours. Among the most successful composers of these operas were Attwood, Dibdin, and Shield, whose *Rosina* (1783) may be taken as typical of the form at its best. After Shield it began to decline; with Horn and Kelly it sank to a lower level; with Bishop it became stiff and professorial; but it was always tuneful and light-hearted, and we may well be grateful to any movement which culminated at our own doors in the works of Sir Arthur Sullivan.

Finally, a word should be said to commemorate the two eminent historians of music who flourished during the eighteenth century. They had certain points of association: Hawkins published his five volumes in 1776, Burney the first of his four volumes in the same year: both were intimate friends of Dr. Johnson, who met Burney frequently at Mrs. Thrale's and who appointed Hawkins his executor; both conceived, and one carried out the intention of writing Johnson's biography; both were slow and deliberate workers; Hawkins took sixteen years over his history, Burney describes his as the fruit of thirty years' meditation and twenty years' writing. Here, however, the resemblances end. Hawkins was a wealthy amateur who looked at life mainly through the spectacles of books, and gained the bulk of his materials from the purchase of Dr. Pepusch's library. He was a careful and diligent researcher who left no corner of the subject unexplored, but he had only an amateur's knowledge of music, and he sometimes falls into errors from which he would have been saved by a more intimate acquaintance with the practice of the art. Boswell, who disliked him, speaks of his " solemn inaccuracy," and this verdict, if unduly hostile, is not wholly without justification. But though he needs some revision his work is valuable for its immense industry and its encyclopædic range, and it has won such reputation that in the nineteenth century it has been twice reprinted. Burney, for nine years organist at King's Lynn, was a far better musician, who made his mark as composer both for the stage and for the concert-room, and whose exercise for the Doctorate at Oxford had a considerable vogue both in England and in Germany. From 1770 to 1772 he travelled widely through the Continent, and on return published the results of his investigations in three volumes which are among the most diverting of musical diaries. In 1773 he was elected a Fellow of the Royal Society, and from 1776 to 1789 published at irregular intervals his *General History of Music*, ranging from the earliest times to the Handel Centenary Festival. He was not only a better artist than Hawkins but a more agreeable writer: he is remarkably free from pedantry, his judgments, though clearly on the conservative side, are usually temperate and well-informed, his style so easy, flowing, and dignified that even Walpole,[1] to whom most of the book was Hebrew, could find its pages "not barren of entertainment." His chief fault is a want of perspective which makes him assign too much space to trivial and unimportant composers, especially of opera, and neglects a good many among the great heroes and leaders of the art. He gives an appreciative account of Palestrina; for Purcell he is our chief authority; but he knows little of Byrd,

[1] Letter to Rev. William Mason: 24th February 1776.

dismisses Wilbye in a couple of sentences, and treats Lully with perfunctory disdain. Most astonishing is his omission of J. S. Bach, who, when the history appeared, had been dead for over a quarter of a century, but of whom it says nothing except that he was a distinguished organist and that he was held in high repute by Marpurg. Still, in spite of its defects the work is a true classic, and its attitude towards music may be summed up in the closing words, of the irony of which Burney was not perhaps wholly aware:

"Though I have constantly treated old masters with reverence it has never been at the expense of the modern. Indeed respect for the dead should not annihilate all kindness for the living, who are in much greater want of patronage. The artist who is suffered to linger in want and obscurity is made but small amends by posthumous honours and commemoration."

CHAPTER VI

DAWN AND PROGRESS OF THE ENGLISH RENASCENCE

THE success won by Burney and Hawkins encouraged the production of further books on music which appeared in the early part of the nineteenth century, and are still valuable as indicating the taste and judgment of their time. Four of these may here be specially mentioned: the *Autobiography* of Michael Kelly, Lord Mount Edgcumbe's *Musical Reminiscences*, *Music and Friends*, by William Gardiner, and the *Musical History* of George Hogarth. They are not monumental achievements, but they are pleasant and informative, and they contain some significant examples of critical opinion.

Michael Kelly, born at Dublin in 1762, was a famous tenor, who, after winning abundant laurels throughout Italy, settled in Vienna where he enjoyed the friendship and admiration of Mozart. On returning to England he made his way both as singer and as composer, joined forces with Sheridan, and managed for thirty years the Little Theatre in the Haymarket. His "*Autobiography*," written by Theodore Hook, appeared in 1826 and at once went into a second edition. It is a frank and good-humoured account of his career, enlivened with many amusing anecdotes, and containing a full record of our operatic history from 1787 until his retirement from the stage in 1821. With the exception of Burney there is no English writer on music who has been so often quoted.

Lord Mount Edgcumbe's *Reminiscences* deal almost entirely with the opera, though the third and best edition (1834) concludes with an excellent and discriminating account of the Handel Festival given at Westminster in that year. He was born in 1764, was brought up in the society of the wits, and was enough of a musician to have an opera accepted by the King's Theatre. That it was not successful may be inferred partly from the brevity of its run, partly from his rather acid criticism of the management.[1] He writes with the pen of a dilettante: he is more interested in the performer than the composition: but he has a refined and cultivated taste, he is an enthusiast for his subject, and he has some illuminating things to say about the relative merits of *prime donne*, the prevalence of the *pasticcio*, and the disposition of a festival orchestra.

The other two authors are of more general interest. William Gardiner was a Leicestershire stocking-weaver, whose gossiping and discursive autobiography, called *Music and Friends*, was published in 1838 and attracted wide attention. He was an amateur violinist of evident skill and understanding, who had been the first English writer to acclaim the supremacy of Beethoven,[2] and at a time

---

[1] *Reminiscences*, Third Edition, p. 74.
[2] See his note to Bombet's *Haydn and Mozart*, p. 64. The translation to which this was appended is dated 1817. See also *Music and Friends*, p. 364.

when critical opinion was mainly concerned with opera and operatic singers, he had the singularity to express his preference for instrumental music and especially for its most intimate form, the string quartet. On his oratorio of *Judah*, and his other unfortunate adaptations, we need not here dwell: there was true musicianship in the critic who, when even the earliest works of Beethoven were regarded as "wild, crabbed, and unintelligible," could say of the first Rasoumoffsky, "In this composition there is more mind than can be found in a hundred pages of any other author."

Last, and most important, is Dickens' father-in-law, George Hogarth, who began his career as an Edinburgh law-student and ended it on the staff of the *Daily News*. The *History* by which his name is chiefly known, was printed in 1855, and though unjustly depreciated by Fétis, remains a sound and valuable contribution to our musical literature. As might be expected it is largely occupied with the products of our own country about which it gives us some useful contemporary information: as, for instance, the great advance in music publishing which took place in the early nineteenth century: the readiness of the English to accept native opera when they could get it,[1] the preference of Weber for English over Italian singers, and two passages on the cultivation of music in Northern England which are worth quoting entire:

"In the densely populated manufacturing districts of Yorkshire, Lancashire and Derbyshire,

[1] See a very remarkable passage to this effect on p. 431.

music is cultivated among the working-classes to an extent unparalleled in any other part of the kingdom."

And again:

"Every village church has its occasional holiday oratorio; the employers promote and encourage so salutary a recreation by countenancing and contributing to defray the expenses of these associations; and some great manufacturers provide regular musical instruction for such of their workpeople as show a disposition for it."[1]

And it was not only in the north of England that a need of musical education began to urge. Gardiner, writing in 1817, expresses a popular feeling when he complains that

"Although more money is expended on music in England than in any other country in Europe, we have no national establishment for the study of the art";

and it was to remove this reproach that in 1822-3 the Royal Academy of Music was established in London. George IV accepted the office of chief patron, Crotch was appointed principal, among the professors were Attwood, Shield, and Sir George Smart, among the external teachers Cramer, Anfossi, Dragonetti, and Cipriani Potter. Clementi, though now over seventy, was induced to take some of the pianoforte classes, and was followed a couple of years later by Moscheles: altogether a ministry of

[1] Hogarth, *Musical History, Biography, and Criticism*, pp. 430-1.

many talents in whose government there was every promise of artistic success. After a short period of the vicissitudes which every new institution may be expected to confront, the Academy settled itself on a firm basis: in 1830 it obtained its charter, and from that time forth its career was assured. We may add that among its earlier pupils was a choir-boy named Sterndale Bennett, who entered it in 1825 and who was destined to exercise a very considerable influence on the English music of the nineteenth century.

Bennett was indeed one of the two composers— John Field the other—who restored our music after a hundred years' exile to a place in the comity of European civilization. They were widely different in character and fortunes: one correct to the point of precision, the other idle and self-indulgent; one loaded with offices and distinctions, the other rescued by bare accident from a pauper's grave; but their talents were genuine and their voices broke the silence by which our native art had for so long been enveloped.

John Field[1] (1782-1837), was the son of an Irish violinist. After a childhood of misery and ill-usage he was brought by his father to London and engaged as salesman to Clementi's pianoforte warehouse. Clementi noticed his ability, gave him piano lessons, and in 1802 took him on a tour through France, Germany, and Russia, in which he won great renown especially as a player of Bach. In Germany he met Spohr, who prophesied a brilliant future for him;[2] in

---

[1] See "John Field," by Eric Blom, *Chesterian*, June-August 1930.
[2] Spohr, *Autobiography*, vol. i, p. 43.

Russia he was so successful that he determined to
settle in that country. Then followed the brightest
and happiest period of his life: he was in high repute
both as teacher and as performer, he married, he
wrote some of his most notable compositions; one
would say that the door of opportunity had never
stood wider open. We do not know how the
downfall came or how gradual was the descent. He
left Russia, wandered back to London and thence to
Paris, where in 1832 he enjoyed a brief period of
triumph, and the rest is an unhappy record of failing
powers and waning popularity. He travelled for a
time through Belgium, Switzerland, and Italy, but
his concerts, at first successful, gradually fell into
neglect, and under the strain his health finally gave
way. In 1836 he was discovered, penniless, in a
common hospital at Naples, by a Russian family who
remembered the old days, and took him home with
them. He reached Moscow at the end of the year
and in January 1837 he died.

His compositions include four sonatas, seven
concertos, of great reputation in their time, a piano
quintet and a number of miscellaneous pieces. But
his title to immortality rests on the collection of
eighteen nocturnes, tender and delicate idylls of
which he is said to have invented both the title and
the form. They are so intimate that Fétis doubts
whether they were intended for publication: if so
Field was well advised to alter his intention for they
became at once famous throughout Europe. There
can be no doubt that they profoundly influenced
Chopin, who was in Paris when most of them
appeared, and whose nocturnes, especially the first,

second, tenth, and fourteenth, often resemble them in transparence of style and sweetness of melody.[1] We are told that they were irresistible when their composer played them: even now in sympathetic hands they can yield something of their old charm and fragrance. It is needless to say that they never attain to the colour and romance of Chopin's most characteristic work:—the mystery of the sixth nocturne, the passion of the seventh, the magic of the twelfth;—they are still further from the Chopin who wrote the "Preludes," the "Etudes," and the "B♭ minor sonata": but in their kind they are as distinctive as they are melodious, and they fill with honour the narrow limits of their achievement. "Mon verre n'est pas grand," he might have said with Alfred de Musset, "mais je bois dans mon verre."

Shortly after the time when Field relinquished his career as a teacher, Sterndale Bennett, then a child of nine, came to London and entered the Royal Academy. He was born in 1816, the son of a Sheffield organist, and showed early a degree of talent surprising even in the most precocious of all the arts. A pianoforte concerto written when he was seventeen, caught the notice of Mendelssohn, who warmly commended him and offered to take him to Germany. This offer he was obliged, for reasons of poverty, to decline, but in 1836, by which time he had written two more concertos and the overtures to *Parisina* and *The Naiads*, the generosity of Messrs.

[1] Rellstab, the Berlin critic, compared Field's nocturnes with Chopin's to the disadvantage of the latter, and though it is an unfair and partisan article the fact of comparison is significant. Field's first nocturnes were published in 1814: Chopin's appeared from 1833 onwards.

Broadwood enabled him to pay his long-deferred visit and he set out for Leipzig full of confidence and expectation. The event exceeded his utmost hopes: he was welcomed by Mendelssohn and Schumann, admitted to the inner circle of the Gewandhaus, and acclaimed by the public with an enthusiasm in which there was possibly intermingled some element of surprise. Schumann led, in the *Neue Zeitschrift*, the chorus of praise: the other critics swelled it to fuller volume: within a few months this shy, retiring boy of twenty-one had become an international hero. The next few years were divided between England and Germany: in 1840 he produced the "F minor Concerto" in London and *The Wood-Nymphs* overture at Leipzig; in 1849 he founded our Bach Society, of which he was the first president; in 1853 he was offered the conductorship of the Gewandhaus concerts, a very signal honour for an English musician, which, though sorely tempted, he felt himself obliged to decline. Thenceforward his career was marked by a series of official dignities and appointments: among others the conductorship of the Philharmonic, the Chair of Music at Cambridge, and the Principalship of the Royal Academy. He was knighted in 1871, and died, the acknowledged head of English music, in 1875.

What does it all mean? How has it come that the artist whom Schumann heralded as a master, and Mendelssohn as a "true genius,"[1] is by his fellow-

---

[1] See his letter of 17th December 1843, quoted s.v. Mendelssohn in the first edition of Grove, vol. ii, p. 283. There is not one among Mendelssohn's contemporaries of whom he speaks with a warmer admiration.

countrymen either ignored or treated with a half-patronizing tolerance? Two explanations may be offered. The first is that almost all his best work was written before he was twenty-five. For the last forty years of his life he was overwhelmed with administration duties—as teacher, as conductor, as principal of a great institution: and under their weight his genius faltered and sank until it was all but crushed out of existence. The first three overtures—*Parisina, The Naiads,* and *The Wood-Nymphs*—are in their kind masterly: so are the early concertos, especially those in D minor and F minor. The contrast is lamentable when we come to his later writings—"The May Queen," "The G minor Symphony," "The Woman of Samaria"—there is something left of the old skill, and all of the old sincerity, but the freshness of inspiration is gone: it is tired work, "numbers ratified" and the "golden cadence of poetry" is wanting. Hence if we would judge him fairly we must concentrate attention on the compositions which he wrote when he was young and unfettered, not on those oases of scanty leisure which lie scattered in a desert of overwork. The gratitude of man has often left its recipient mourning: there is no more pathetic example than that of a genius whose art, forced into reluctant harness, was broken down by the burden of its own reward. And as the first reason is attributable to Bennett's disastrous good fortune so the second springs from a remarkable want of discrimination in ourselves. By a curious perversity we have thrust into the dark those compositions which are most worthy of our attention, and allowed a feeble glimmer to rest upon

those with which we could most readily dispense:
two of the latter are kept in suspended animation
by amateur choral societies in search of an easy task:
of the former we are content to accept disparaging
accounts at second hand from critics who have not
always understood their business. It is, for instance,
a common judgment that Bennett's music is a copy
of Mendelssohn's—that he is a weaker Mendelssohn
as Field is an immature Chopin. How anyone can
say this who knows the overtures and the concertos
it is difficult to comprehend. They sometimes recall
for a moment a Mendelssohnian turn of phrase, but
so far as they are derivative it is Mozart from whom
they draw their origin and by whom their style is
chiefly affected. Indeed one of the reasons why they
are out of favour with our concert-soloists is that
their technique, like that of Mozart, gives more
scope for interpretation than opportunity of
display.

It is no disparagement of Sterndale Bennett to
say that he was a water-colourist: that the essential
qualities of his work are its transparence, its even-
ness, and its skill of draughtsmanship. If these
qualities attract us we shall find them abundantly in
such works as the F minor Concerto[1] or *The Wood-
Nymphs* overture: if we want vehemence and passion
and glowing canvass we had better look elsewhere.
There was a day in 1856 when the conductorship of
the Philharmonic changed hands: the baton assumed
by Bennett had been laid down by Richard Wagner.
It was a striking contrast—a gentle and graceful
talent against a tempestuous and overwhelming

[1] See Illustration K.

genius. The two men belong to different orders, to different worlds: there can be no point of comparison between them, and it was but a moment's irony which brought them into contact. Yet though the higher ranges of art were closed to Bennett he has an honourable place on the mid-slopes: he found English music a barren land, he enriched its soil, developed its cultivation, and adorned it with blossoms of his native eglantine.

We have seen that he owed much to the encouragement of Mendelssohn with whom, both here and in Germany, he had many opportunities of close relationship. Mendelssohn, who had a great affection for this country, visited us ten times between 1829 and 1847: he wrote *The Hebrides* here, he produced here the Italian symphony, the *Lobgesang*, the *Antigone*, and the *Elijah*, he gave us early performances of *St. Paul* and the Scotch Symphony. His personal attractiveness and his astonishing musical gifts gained him a large company of friends and admirers: the *Lobgesang* was received with an ovation, the *Elijah* then and for many years afterwards rivalled Handel in popularity. He had indeed an appeal for every one: a master of ready and somewhat facile emotion, supreme in delicacy and humour, a craftsman who never wasted a tool or missed an effect, he charmed the virtuosi with his concertos, the public with his oratorios and the domestic circle with his lyrics. He influenced many of our composers for a generation after his death: his best work is of unimpeachable value, and we are still glad to remember the welcome which he received at our hands. It is only the Prigsbys who "never listen to Mendelssohn because there are no wrong notes."

Another English writer whom both Mendelssohn and Schumann befriended was Hugo Pierson. He was the son of a clergyman who ultimately became Dean of Salisbury, was educated at Harrow and Trinity Cambridge, and in 1844 was elected to the Reid Professorship at Edinburgh—Sterndale Bennett and Wesley being two of the defeated candidates. Next year he resigned his office on some punctilio, and settled in Germany, where he remained for the rest of his life. His incidental music to Goethe's *Faust* won him considerable reputation, but his name has now faded and he is no longer of any serious account. Nor, with one notable exception, is there much to occupy us in the other composers of the half century. Pearsall revived the madrigal, and wrote some interesting examples; Hatton and Loder made some mark as song-writers; Bishop spread his academic robes over the theatre; Balfe, his exact antithesis, gained a hearing for the cornet-solos of *The Bohemian Girl.* But in the Church there was still some continuity of tradition: Attwood to Walmisley, Walmisley to Goss and Henry Smart: Macfarren aided the cause with tireless industry, Ouseley with high ideals and generous support, all in their way furthering an advance which attained its height in the person of Samuel Sebastian Wesley.

A son of Samuel Wesley, whose gifts he inherited and whose opportunities he bettered, he spent his whole life in the service of the English Church: first as chorister at the Chapel Royal, then in various

London parishes, then as organist successively of
Hereford, Exeter, Leeds, Winchester, and Gloucester. His crabbedness and eccentricity, of which
many stories are told, were chiefly due to an abnor-
mal sensitiveness of ear: he could detect the tiniest
nuances of organ-colour, he was distressed even by
the practical compromise of equal temperament.
As performer and improviser there had been no one
like him since the days of Handel, and the brilliance
and readiness of invention which he showed at the
keyboard inspired in full measure the quality of his
composition. In his early days English taste was
largely dominated by Spohr, of whose influence we
may find some traces in "The Wilderness," and
especially in its closing chorus: his more mature
work is freed from all trammels of discipleship and
speaks unmistakably with its own voice and its own
language. In 1845 he wrote his great Service in
E major, and published it with a vigorous and
outspoken preface on the deplorable state of Church
music at the time. In 1853 followed the monumental
collection of twelve anthems on which his fame
principally rests. At Gloucester, where he was
appointed in 1865, he was too deeply engaged with
his clergy and his choir to have much leisure for
composition: the omens on both sides were unfavourable, for the chief objects of his detestation
were Deans, Precentors, and Music Publishers. In
1872 he edited *The European Psalmist*, to which he
contributed some of his finest tunes, in 1875 he
accompanied at the cathedral for the last time. Next
year, at the age of sixty-six, he died. His published
works include some five and twenty anthems, four

services, and a number of chants, hymns, and miscellaneous pieces.

It is the easier to appraise his work because all that is important hangs in one gallery. "The Wilderness" and "Blessed be the God and Father" belong to his early days at Hereford and were not yet welded into complete unity of form, but they contain some beautiful numbers—notably the radiant chorus, "For in the wilderness shall waters break out," and the splendid and jubilant outburst, "But the word of the Lord endureth for ever." From these he advanced in strength and dignity, in firmness of design and richness of harmonic colour, in a dignity which ranks him with the classics and an intimacy of feeling which brings him very close to ourselves. Take, for instance, "Ascribe unto the Lord," with its contrast of disdain for the gods of the heathen who are but idols, and of serene confidence in "Our God who is in Heaven." Take the pathos of "Wash me throughly,"[1] and the tenderness of "Thou wilt keep him in perfect peace": the fervour of "Thou judge of quick and dead": the sublimity of "O God thou art my God," a work which, in Dannreuther's phrase, "should be studied and recognized as masterly wherever the English language is spoken." He has the gift, possessed by those alone who stand in the inner courts, of making music which at first surprises us by its novelty and afterwards convinces us that it was inevitable: he leads us into paths hitherto untrodden and opens the way by which we can follow. He was original without extravagance, lucid without shallowness;

[1] See Illustration L.

in a dark period he lightened our English liturgy with a lamp that will long endure.

It is not claimed for these three men—Field, Bennett, and Wesley—that they were more than "little masters." Their range was too restricted and their achievement too slender to rank them among the *di majorum gentium*. But it is claimed that they were artists who had pure treasure to bestow and that, apart from conditions of time and circumstance, their names occupy a place in our roll of honour. There are many parallels from English poetry: Wyatt wrote but little, so did Waller, so did Gray and Collins, yet we have no misgivings about "Forget not yet," or "Go, lovely rose," or the "Elegy," or the "Ode to Evening." Inspiration is not less real in those whom it rarely visits: its quality may be enhanced by largeness and generosity of expression, but in its least manifestations it is unmistakable.

The advance which was tentatively begun in the first half of the nineteenth century continued during the second with increased strength and sureness. A landmark was passed in 1861 when Arthur Sullivan, then a boy of nineteen, produced at the Crystal Palace his incidental music to *The Tempest* and stepped at once into the forefront of public favour. He was the son of an Irish bandmaster, born in London, and educated at the Chapel Royal, the Academy, and the Leipzig Conservatorium; a pupil in England of Goss and Bennett, and in Germany of Moscheles, Rietz, and Moritz Hauptmann. Within a few months of his return he had made a reputation which extended far beyond the capital: during the next ten years even his industry was hard pressed by the volume of his appointments and commissions. Among these the most important in its after effects was the organistship of Covent Garden, which he obtained at the recommendation of Costa in 1864, and which gave him that practical experience of the stage which he was to turn later to such good account. But he held in addition the organistship of two London churches, and the conductorship of two London orchestras, he edited "Church Hymns," he taught, with some reluctance, at the Royal Academy; and all the while came a ceaseless flow of compositions—a cantat for Birmingham, an oratorio for Worcester, an overture for the Philharmonic and another for the Norwich festival, an "Irish" symphony, a violoncello concerto, a few essays in dramatic writing, and a vast number of popular songs.

All these, however, in our general estimate of his works, are but side issues. The Sullivan who has written his name across English music is the composer not of "Kenilworth" or "The Prodigal Son," still less of "The Lost Chord" and "Onward, Christian soldiers," but of the Comic Operas with which for over thirty years he added to the gaiety of nations. In them he found his true *métier*; the appropriate field for his gifts of melody and humour and stage effect: they are in their kind classics and it is by them that his name is held in remembrance.

He began with three trial flights, *Cox and Box*, *La Contrabandista*, and *Thespis*, in two of which he was hampered by a bad librettist and in the third by an uncongenial subject. The real partnership began

in 1875 when *Trial by Jury* made the names of Gilbert
and Sullivan into household words, and thenceforward its welcome was assured and continuous.
In 1877 *The Sorcerer* was produced at the opening of
D'Oyly Carte's new theatre, and then followed in
succession *Pinafore*, *The Pirates of Penzance*, *Patience*
(the only one wholly occupied with contemporary
satire), *Iolanthe*, *Princess Ida*, the least successful of the
series, *The Mikado*, which did more than compensate,
Ruddigore, which contains some of Sullivan's best
music, *The Yeomen of the Guard*, favourite both of
author and composer, and so through *The Gondoliers*,
Utopia Limited, and *The Grand Duke*, which appeared
in 1896 and on which the two collaborators joined
hands for the last time. In the whole history of the
operatic stage there had been no such acclama-
tion. *The Pirates* and *Patience* ran for over 400
nights apiece, *The Mikado* for 675, *Patience* for
700. The production of each was hailed as an
event of almost national importance, the course of
each continued until the time was ready for its
successor. Nor was this only a matter of temporary
and transitory fashion. Sullivan's melody has endeared itself to the heart of every Englishman.
Gilbert's whimsical humour has added a new word
to the English language.

Many artists would have been satisfied with a
triumph so complete, but Sullivan seems to have
desired something more brocaded and ceremonial.
Possibly he felt it due to his position or yielded to the
solicitations of friends; possibly he misjudged his
powers, like Gilbert, whose chief ambition, we are
told, was to excel in tragedy:—whatever the reason

he occasionally diverged from his true path and trod once more the less familiar ways of cantata and oratorio. In 1873 he wrote *The Light of the World* for Birmingham, in 1880 *The Martyr of Antioch* for Leeds; in 1886, again at Leeds, he produced a long and elaborate setting of Longfellow's *Golden Legend.* That these had their measure and period of success is unquestionable—their composer's name was itself a guarantee—but they are not the real Sullivan: apart from a few picturesque passages they have no enduring quality: they are but episodes in a career which they interrupted rather than enhanced. A more congenial, because a more natural ambition, is commemorated by his one adventure into Grand Opera. As we can see from *The Yeomen of the Guard,* he had a genuine, though not very deep feeling for romance. Two years after its appearance the opening of a new opera house gave him further opportunity, and he accepted a commission to write its inaugural work. The result was *Ivanhoe,* which in 1891 was magnificently produced and very cordially received. But the scheme of organization was over-hazardous from the outset: then, as now, English opera had no subsidy on which to rely, the expenses were enormous, the promoters were faced with bankruptcy; after a run of 160 nights *Ivanhoe* was withdrawn, and shortly afterwards the house was sold to the syndicate of a music-hall.

Sullivan returned to the familiar security of light opera, and during the last years of his life wrote in that form five more works, the most notable being *The Rose of Persia* (1899) in which for the first time since the breach with Gilbert he had the advantage of an amusing and sympathetic librettist. But he was now working under great physical disability. A distressing and painful disease to which he had been subject all his life was steadily encroaching; in 1898 he felt obliged to resign his last public appointment; in 1900 he died at the early age of fifty-eight, and was buried amid a vast concourse of mourners in St. Paul's Cathedral.

It has been said that he was lucky in his chief collaborator: it should be added that no man ever more thoroughly deserved his luck. The two arts are here fused into a sympathy so complete that we can hardly separate them: they are like convex and concave, "two in name, one in reality." If it was Gilbert who devised the fantastic plots it was Sullivan who illuminated them; if we owe to Gilbert the close-knit economy of stagecraft,[1] we owe to Sullivan the variety with which it was embroidered. The music is as witty as the verse and has the same ease and deftness. It is unnecessary to search at length for illustrations; there is hardly an opera but has added to our store some irresistible jest or some charm of melody. The banqueting chorus from *The Sorcerer*, the "Willow waley" duet from *Patience*, the "Flowers that bloom in the spring" from *The Mikado*, the "Merriman" song from *The Yeomen of the Guard*; each name suggests a dozen other delights of humour and tunefulness and masterly orchestration. Only in some of the sentimental

---

[1] "It is perhaps amusing to reflect," says Mr. G. K. Chesterton, (*The Eighteen-eighties*, p. 149), "that the author of the *Bab Ballads* was the only Englishman who understood and observed the unities of the Greek Tragedy."

numbers does the quality of the music seem for a moment to decline, and this not for want of spontaneity but through a certain softness of temperament which was Sullivan's principal defect. And it is the good fortune of the operas that they afford less scope for this than he found in his more serious works. A distinguished foreign critic, cited by Mr. Chesterton, has summed up the general testimony in words which we may all cordially endorse: "It would be easy," he says, "to find here and there, on the Continent, one or two comic operas as good or better: but of the Savoy Operas there are at least ten, if not twelve, of the first rank of invention." "And," he adds, "we had come to count on their going on for ever like the seasons of summer or of spring."

Sullivan, as we know, disliked teaching, but he was rewarded for its drudgery by the success of at least one among his pupils. This was Arthur Goring Thomas (1850-1892), whose *Esmeralda*, produced in 1883, may be counted as the greatest of English romantic operas. It was at once repeated in Cologne and Hamburg, it was translated into French and reappeared, in that guise, at Covent Garden; its dexterous and polished music is well worth reviving at the present day. In 1885 followed *Nadeshda*, which exhibits the same qualities on a smaller scale, and which contains a choral ballet of great merit. He was considerably influenced by French music, especially by Bizet, but he wore his rue with a difference, and his best music is memorable both for daintiness of imagination and for skill of treatment.

The overflowing success of the Royal Academy led during this period to the establishment of other schools and colleges in London. Chief among these were, in order of date, the Royal College of Organists, which was founded in 1864 and gained its charter in 1893, the National Training School, founded in 1873 with Sullivan for its first Principal, the Guildhall School which followed, under Weist Hill, in 1879, and the Royal College of Music which in 1882 took over the work of the National Training School and was established as a separate institution under the directorship of Sir George Grove. To these were added in due course municipal schools like those of Manchester and Birmingham; the universities began to reorganize and develop their musical resources, the public school came gradually into line; little by little a higher place was found for musical education not only as professional training but as an element in humane letters. These reforms met with a ready welcome. Choral and orchestral societies grew in strength and popularity; the competition festivals, begun in 1885, carried the example of the Welsh Eisteddfodau[1] through the length and breadth of the country, everywhere came signs of an awakening for which the course of the mid-century had made its due preparation.[2]

Round about 1880 the new chapter was opened. In that year Parry wrote his "Prometheus" and Cowen his Scandinavian Symphony; in 1881 Stanford wrote "The Veiled Prophet," and followed it with the Elegiac Symphony in 1882. Next year

[1] It is noticeable that the name Eisteddfod means literally "an assemblage of learned men."
[2] A general sketch of the state of music in England was written as a report to the Carnegie Trustees in 1921.

came Mackenzie's orchestral ballad, "La belle dame sans merci," which in the opinion of many critics is his finest work. And in the band of the three-choir festivals, at this time, was a young violinist named Elgar, already known as a writer of slight and fugitive pieces, and about to enter, with his overture "Froissart," the front rank of English composition.

Mackenzie, the eldest of the group, was born at Edinburgh in 1845. His early career was spent partly as a student in Germany and London, partly as a violinist in the Birmingham Festival orchestra, where he gained a practical experience that afterwards stood him in good stead. In 1879 he was ordered abroad for reasons of health, and during the next ten years resided principally at Florence, returning from time to time in order to fulfil engagements or produce compositions. In 1888 he succeeded Sir George Macgarren at the Academy, the fortunes of which he directed with equal wisdom and devotion for no less than thirty-six years. Beside his work there as teacher and administrator he conducted for some years the Royal Choral Society and the Philharmonic; in 1903 he undertook an extensive tour in Canada and founded there a number of schools and societies; on his return he was appointed president of the *Internationale Musikgesellschaft*, and in that capacity guided two of its conferences—Vienna in 1909, London in 1911. At the age of seventy-nine he gave up his public work and has since then lived in retirement. He has been the recipient of many honours, national as well as academic. There is no aspect of our musical life which has not benefited by his influence and example.

A career so fully occupied with administrative problems has naturally been hampered in the fields of composition, and though Mackenzie's published works approach the number of one hundred, it is not surprising that the best of them belong to his years of comparative freedom. We have already noted "La belle dame sans merci" as a landmark: hardly less distinctive are "The Rose of Sharon," produced at Norwich in 1884, the Violin Concerto of 1885, the Pibroch Suite (1886), "The Cottar's Saturday Night" (1892), and in their finest numbers the early Scottish Rhapsodies and the operas of *Colomba* and *The Troubadour*. From thenceforward the stream begins to run more tardily through the sands of office, and though it recalls for a moment its former clearness in the third "Scottish Rhapsody" of 1911, it tells too often our familiar story of a talent "shorn and parcelled" by the very diversities of its employment. In him therefore as in Bennett (and for the same reason) it is to the earlier writings that we must look for the qualities which have won him his place in our national music. Chief among them is a warmth of imagination which, if never passionate, is moving and sympathetic, and which may be illustrated by the Pibroch Suite, the orchestral ballad above mentioned, and the more "Romantic" numbers of "The Rose of Sharon." To this may be added, on the technical side, his command of orchestral effect, particularly of the violin, which he always handles with intimate knowledge and understanding. It is curious that with all his predilection for Scottish themes his own style and idiom are not especially nationalist: he is not Scottish in the sense in which Parry is English or Stanford Irish: his range of expression is less concentrated and more cosmopolitan. But his originality is beyond question, and if it failed to sustain its early promise it has made to our national music a contribution of real and lasting value.

Mackenzie was succeeded at the Philharmonic by F. H. Cowen, another composer who began his career as a virtuoso. He was born in Jamaica (1852) and educated at Leipzig and Berlin, from which he returned in 1868, a skilful and accomplished pianist. He made his début as a composer in 1869 when he produced at St. James's Hall a symphony and a pianoforte concerto: in 1880 he wrote the "Scandinavian Symphony," which rapidly made its way in England, in America, and on the Continent. The success of this work enabled him to give up his career as an executant and to follow the more congenial occupation of composer and conductor, in both of which he attained great popularity. Among his published works are six symphonies, and four overtures, four operas, seven oratorios, and a number of cantatas, smaller orchestral pieces and songs. His work is always deft and light-handed: he excels in fairy music and in sentiment lightly uttered: at his best he rises to real daintiness of fancy, at his worst he sinks to triviality and commonplace. Among the five musicians whom we are here considering he is of least account, but he had his day, and if the achievement has faded the memory still remains.

Parry and Stanford are associated in the fields of

music as in the fields of politics are Pitt and Fox, or Disraeli and Gladstone: each is the complement and enhancement of the other. They were close contemporaries. Parry born in 1848, Stanford in 1852, they came into prominence as composers at about the same time; for over thirty years they worked together at the Royal College: each held the chair of music at one of our older universities. To them our national music owed more than to any man since Purcell, and, with the exception of Purcell, to any man since Byrd. In the first maturity of our renaissance they held a leadership as supreme as it was unquestioned.

Parry was the son of a Gloucestershire squire and was educated at Eton and Oxford. In his college days he received some musical instruction from Macfarren, Bennett, and H. H. Pierson: shortly after taking his degree he had the good fortune to meet Edward Dannreuther with whom he formed a lifelong friendship, and whose advice and encouragement were at this time invaluable. It was for Dannreuther's musical gatherings at Orme Square that he wrote most of his early chamber work: it was Dannreuther who introduced him to a wider public by playing at the Crystal Palace his early pianoforte concerto, and to the interest which these aroused he owed his invitation to write a choral work for the Gloucester Festival of 1880. It must be said, to our indelible disgrace, that *Prometheus* was not successful. The public was bewildered by its novelty, and looked for guidance to the official critics: these, instigated by an English Beckmesser, ignored its beauties and declared against it. But a second performance at Oxford did something to repair the error; good opinion was strengthened in 1883 by an eloquent setting of Shirley's Ode; in 1887 the Bach choir sang "Blest Pair of Sirens," and the victory was complete. From that day until his death there were very few festivals which did not contain at least one of his more important works. "St. Cecilia" in 1889, "L'Allegro ed Il Penseroso" in 1890, the "De Profundis" in 1891, "The Lotus Eaters" and "Job" in 1892, the "Magnificat" in 1897, the motets from 1903 onwards, the exquisite "Songs of Farewell" which occupied his later years: these are but the peaks of a range of undying strength and beauty. And round them, like meadows in the foothills, are over a hundred lyrics, grave and gay by turn, and full of charm and melody and poetic insight.

He wrote in all forms except opera, for which, like Brahms, he had no taste.[1] His instrumental work, with the exception possibly of the Symphonic Variations and certainly of the organ preludes, is of secondary account: it is firm and dignified, it contains no cheap effect and no unworthy phrase, but it has not the sense of colour and contrast on which orchestral writing so much depends, and it holds so far aloof from sensationalism that it even discountenances adventure. His chief strength, and here he has no rival throughout our history, is his gift of entering into the very heart of noble poetry, not by the reflected light of illustration or comment but by

---

[1] A boyish opera on Guinevere was found in MS. among his papers. But he trod no further in that path, and by the end of his life had come to regard operatic writing with aversion.

a glow of inspiration which has been kindled at the same fire. A striking example may be found in "Blest Pair of Sirens." The orchestral prelude and the interludes are but pieces of good draughtsmanship, an academic exercise with more learning than imagination: from the moment when the voices enter their music rises through ascent after ascent to a climax of sublimity where it stands, a fitting companion, beside Milton himself. The other great choral writings are illuminated by a like sympathy and understanding: "The Lotus Eaters," for instance, and the "De Profundis" and the "Songs of Farewell": the choruses of "Prometheus," the Orpheus music of "St. Cecilia," the Dirge of the Purcell Ode. These are indeed a Testament of Beauty; high in aim, stately in expression, and informed with a spirit which is of the very life and breath of our people.[1]

Stanford, the son of an examiner in the Court of Chancery, was born at Dublin and bred up to music first under Sir Robert Stewart and later under Reinecke at Leipzig and Kiel at Berlin. From 1873 to 1892 he was organist of Trinity College, Cambridge, where he did admirable service as conductor of the University Musical Society. On the opening of the Royal College he was appointed by Grove to the chair of composition, a post which he held continuously until his death. His other public offices may be briefly summarised. From 1885 to 1892 he was conductor of the Bach Choir, in 1887 he became Professor of Music at Cambridge, in 1901 he succeeded Sullivan as conductor of the Leeds

[1] See Illustration M.

Festival. To all these he brought untiring energy and efficiency: he reorganized the Cambridge musical degree, he was a first-rate conductor, he long enjoyed the reputation of being the best teacher in Europe. Indeed many of the leading composers of the next generation—Charles Wood, Arthur Somervell, Vaughan Williams, Walford Davies, Rutland Boughton—passed through his hands and profited by his influence.

But his true life, like that of Parry, is to be found in his compositions. He was an abundant and prolific writer, some two hundred of whose works are catalogued in Grove, and his long experience as a teacher ripened in him a skill and felicity of style which is the mature fruit of scholarship. "Reading," says Bacon, "maketh a full man, conference a ready man," and Stanford possessed both qualities in a high degree. All his writing gives the impression of ease, of a material under control, of an eloquence which never hesitates for a word or uses a wrong one. He might have said, with Browning's Andrea del Sarto:

> "I can do with my pencil what I know,
> What I see, what at bottom of my heart
> I wish for, if I ever wish so deep."

And again:

> "I do what many dream of all their lives.
> Dream? Strive to do and agonise to do
> And fail in doing."

Such a gift, no doubt, brings its attendant danger. A knowledge so wide and so readily at command

may sometimes "vibrate in the memory" and lead
not only to apposite quotations but to the momen-
tary adoption of another man's general style or idiom.
This is especially likely with a temperament so
sensitive and receptive as that of Stanford. The
overture to *Œdipus Tyrannus*, for example, owes
something to Wagner, the *Stabat Mater* to Verdi,
there is a notable quotation from Brahms in *The
Revenge*, and from Corelli in *Much Ado about Nothing*.
It is no question of plagiarism, the resemblances are
almost certainly unconscious, but they are none the
less present and one need not be a "reminiscence-
hunter" to discern them. They are the more remarkable because they lie so entirely on the surface.
Stanford was at heart inherently and intensely
nationalist, never more happy than when he was
inspired by his native land: his most characteristic
pieces are the "Irish Symphony" and the "Irish
Rhapsodies," "Phaudrig Crohoore" and "Shamus
O'Brien"; the songs from Leinster and from the glens
of Antrim. In all his work he is a craftsman of almost
uncanny skill: with these and their like he rises
above craftsmanship into the pure serene of poetry.

And it is by these that he will live: not by the
oratorios or the serious operas, or the concertos, or
even such brilliant *tours de force* as the "Eumenides"
and "The Voyage of Maeldunc." *The Revenge* has
deservedly won public favour, so have the "Songs
of the Sea," so has one at least of the Church services; but the changes of modern music, with which
he was wholly unsympathetic, are already making
them seem old-fashioned and they have not the
strength and endurance of his chief contemporary.

Still, when all deductions have been made, he was a great leader, an artist of rare gifts and rare accomplishment, a true pioneer who helped by his genius to secure our advance and by his example to perpetuate it.

Latest in time among the heroes of our renascence is Elgar, born in 1857 at Worcester, where his father was a music-seller, and organist of the Roman Catholic Church. He was virtually self-taught, except for a few violin lessons from Pullitzer, but he had the run of a good library and was brought up from childhood in the study and practice of music. He acquired his knowledge of form by assiduous reading, his command of instrumental colour by deputising for his father, by playing in a local wind-quintet and by successively accompanying and conducting a couple of local orchestras: before the end of the 'eighties he had won, among his own people, a reputation both as violinist and as composer. In 1890 he stepped into a wider area by producing his overture, "Froissart," at a Worcester Festival. The work was given in unfavourable circumstances, but it at once attracted the notice of musicians, and opened the way towards further opportunities—"The Black Knight" and "The Bavarian Highlands" in 1893, "King Olaf" and "The Light of the World" in 1896, and in 1897 "The Banner of St. George," which though musically less important is historically interesting as giving scope both to Elgar's patriotic feeling and his love of pageantry and display.

Both these found fuller expression when in 1898 *Caractacus* was produced at Leeds, and at once gave

Elgar his rank as a composer of national account. It is not a flawless work, it holds an uncertain balance between the methods of cantata and opera, it has not yet shaken off the immaturities of youth, its poetry sometimes degenerates into rhetoric, but its defects are more than counterbalanced by its brilliance and originality, by its picturesqueness of colour and its eloquence of expression. Its weaker numbers are the last of Elgar's apprenticeship; the stronger place him, beyond cavil, among the mastersingers.

In the next year came two works which set their seal on the maturity of his powers: "Sea Pictures" at a Norwich festival, the "Enigma" Variations for Orchestra, played under Richter at St. James's Hall. The latter are so called because of their theme the accompaniment alone is given: each variation bears the initials of a friend and is offered half in jest as a delineation of his character. Into these problems we need no longer enquire: the music speaks for itself and is better without these appeals to our curiosity. It is of all Elgar's writings the one which most closely touches perfection; its beauty of sound, its warmth of colour, its variety of mood, its splendid and unerring orchestration have set it far above criticism and have made it one of the permanent treasures of our country.

Then followed the period of the great oratorios: *Gerontius* in 1900, *The Apostles* and *The Kingdom* (originally intended as part of the same work) in 1903 and 1906.[1] The first of these was not over well

---

[1] We are told that Elgar's scheme of oratorio was planned as a trilogy, the third number of which has not yet appeared, though (*tandem veniat*) it is said to be approaching completion.

received: chorus and public alike were baffled by the
new idiom, the critics took irrelevant exception to
its theology—one even complained of its tendency
to Romanism—John Bull, in short, hesitated to
applaud the strain which he so little understood. It
was not until its triumphant performance at the
Lower Rhine Festival of 1902 that we learned to
recognize it as a masterpiece and to give a more
suitable welcome to its two successors. No doubt in
a composition of such scale and magnitude there may
be room for predilections; but there should have
been no question, as there is none now, about the
hymn "Praise to the Holiest," or the pathos of the
death-scene, or the mystic beauty of the ascent
towards the Throne: and though the other oratorios
are unequal, especially in some of their closing
choruses, their topmost heights are among the stars.
Witness the solemn prelude to *The Kingdom* in which
the highest utterance of Elgar's religious music is
gathered and consummated.[1]

Meantime other compositions were interspersed—
the *Cockagne* and *Alassio* overtures of 1901, the
"Coronation Ode" of 1902, the "Introduction and
Allegro for Strings," which recalled to a different
purpose the old forces of the Concerto Grosso. In
1905 he was appointed to the Chair of Music at
Birmingham, but he was wholly unsuited to administrative or academic work, and after three years'
tenure he resigned his office. The new-won freedom
was signalized by an outburst of orchestral composition: the two Symphonies, the Violin Concerto
and "Falstaff" all appeared between 1908 and 1913;

[1] See Illustration N.

and all worthily maintained his reputation. During the War he wrote three short pieces—"Carillon," "To Women," and "For the Fallen"; the last a work of striking beauty and originality. At its close he returned to instrumental forms and produced in rapid succession a violin sonata, a piano quartet, a piano quintet, and a concerto for violoncello. His public services received Royal recognition by his knighthood in 1902, his admission to the Order of Merit in 1911, and the Mastership of the King's Music to which he succeeded Sir Walter Parratt in 1924.

His music is a transition between the old order in which he was brought up and the new to which it gave place. Like Berlioz he was a born revolutionary who owed little to training or tradition and followed in perfect liberty his own genius and his own sense of adventure. But he is a greater man than Berlioz, greater in sustained power of thought, in elevation of sentiment, in dignity and control of expression. The touch of commonplace which may sometimes be noted in his earlier works, is but the *gaucherie* of a man who has not yet learned to be at ease in his surroundings: it has gradually faded as the years brought experience and the foothold grew more secure. And with serenity of manner has come a freedom and variety of utterance which will be a heritage for all our generations to come. He has remodelled the musical language of England: he has enlarged its style and enriched its vocabulary, and the monument of his work is not only a landmark in our present advance but a beacon of guidance for its future.

CHAPTER VII

THE LATER YEARS

THE enlargement of musical idiom, which is so generally characteristic of the present age, came to England later than to any Continental country. It is, indeed, difficult for us to realize that over sixty years have passed since Moussorgsky wrote *Boris* and Dargomijsky *The Stone Guest;* that Dvořák's *Stabat Mater* appeared in 1876 and Franck's *Béatitudes* in 1879: that the symphonic poems of Strauss began in the 'eighties, and that Debussy wrote the *Apres-midi d'un Faune* in 1892: that the latest of these works was contemporary with Sullivan's *Ivanhoe* and the earliest with Bennett's *Woman of Samaria*. There is little need to comment upon this fact, still less to use it as a reason for regret: we are more concerned with tracing the course of English music as it broadened into the main stream of progress and along this flowed into new regions of beauty and adventure.

We shall, then, in this chapter be chiefly occupied with composers the bulk of whose work was written after 1900. But before we come to them, and to the changes which they brought about, we must mention *honoris causa* two members of the older régime to whom, in their several ways, the course of our

musical history has been deeply indebted. Arthur
Somervell, born at Kendal in 1863, first made his
mark as a song-writer of great charm and distinction,
notable not only for his gift of melody but for his
sympathetic understanding of fine poetry, and his
taste and skill in its interpretation. This side of his
work culminated in the "Maud" cycle of 1898, a
true classic, which deservedly stands in the first rank
of English songs. Around this time he was practis-
ing his hand in the larger field of choral composition,
and produced with success a number of odes and
cantatas for the chief provincial festivals: of late he
has turned his attention to instrumental music, and
his more recent compositions, all too few, include a
symphony, a violin concerto, and a set of variations
for pianoforte and orchestra. There are two principal respects in which his influence has been of
inestimable value. He was one of the first men who
drew public attention to our store of national
melodies, and so helped to equip the English
renascence with one of the most potent of its
weapons: and as a Chief Inspector of the Board of
Education he did more than any man in the country
to raise and maintain the standard of music throughout our schools and colleges, substituting for the old
haphazard apathy a reasoned scheme of training with
high ideals and efficient workmanship.

The second name is that of Charles Wood (1866-
1926), a composer whose public reputation is not
yet commensurate with his merits. He was born at
Armagh and educated at the R.C.M., where in 1888
he was appointed to the teaching staff, and where
many generations of pupils can testify to his kind-

ness, his encyclopædic knowledge, and his sensitive
and impeccable taste. During much of his life he
resided at Cambridge as college organist and
university lecturer. At its close he succeeded
Stanford as professor and took official charge of the
university music, which he had done so much to
inspire and stimulate. The paucity of his published
work is due not to barrenness of invention, but to
a self-effacing modesty and a fastidious habit of
self-criticism—the jewels are few in number but they
are of genuine sparkle and faultless workmanship.
They include some half-dozen cantatas and works of
similar scope, a set of symphonic variations, the
incidental music to "Ion," some notable Church
music, of which his service in the Phrygian mode
should be particularly signalized, and six string
quartets published after his death, all of which
maintain a high level of achievement, and one of
which, in A major, deserves a prominent place in
every répertoire of chamber music.

We must be content with the bare record of other
composers who grew up during the latter part of the
nineteenth century and who by temper and predilection belong to the old order. Among them may be
noted Edward German, who wore for a time the
mantle of Sullivan, Hamish M'Cunn, whose "Land
of the Mountain and the Flood" (1887) gained him
a reputation which was afterwards confirmed by
"Lord Ullin's Daughter" and the opera of "Jenny
Deans"; Hurlstone, a writer of delicate and melodious chamber music, whose high promise was cut
short by his death at the age of thirty, and Coleridge
Taylor, an artist in vivid and romantic colouring,

whose "Hiawatha" still claims the welcome with
which it was first received. A more prominent
figure is that of Dame Ethel Smyth, whose "Mass in
D major" (1893) showed a great command of
technical resource and whose operas *Der Wald, The
Wreckers,* and *The Boatswain's Mate* have given her a
high rank among British composers.

So across the turn of the century came a further
stage in the transition from old to new: tentative at
first, as becomes every change in artistic method,
gathering volume and impetus as it proceeded.
One of its earliest leaders was Granville Bantock.
He was born in 1868, educated at the Royal Academy, and after some years of experience as an
opera-conductor, appointed to the musical directorship at New Brighton. There he rendered a service
of national value by organizing concerts of British
music which gave hearing and opportunity to many
of our younger composers and helped to establish
the reputation of the older. In 1900 he took office
at the Midland Institute, Birmingham, and in 1907
succeeded Elgar as Professor at the university. He
is a man of wide and cultivated mind, a keen student
of eastern poetry and philosophy, and a composer of
strong forcible eloquence who moves by predilection in the great spaces and breathes most freely in
the open and larger air. The best known among his
works is the trilogy on Omar Khayyám; not less
valuable are the Hebridean Symphony, "The Great
God Pan," and the two so-called Choral Symphonies, "Atalanta in Calydon" and "Vanity of
Vanities," which are scored for unaccompanied
voices with as firm and exacting a hand as though

they were the massed forces of an orchestra. His fondness for the East has in no way impaired his loyalty to our national music: he has edited and arranged many of our songs and has materially added to our knowledge of the Elizabethans. Altogether he has written some thirty pieces for orchestra, a like number for chorus, a few examples of dramatic music, and the customary collection of songs and smaller pieces. His work is hard to perform, it is sometimes hard to follow, but it is on the epic scale and it amply repays those by whom its difficulties are surmounted.

An almost exact contemporary of Bantock is Walford Davies, born at Oswestry in 1869 and educated at the Royal College of which, in 1895, he joined the teaching staff. His public career began in 1898 when he was appointed organist of the Temple Church, and found there an adequate scope for his remarkable gifts as executant improviser and choir-trainer. His early compositions, both for Church and for chamber, carried his reputation into wider fields, and its recognition rose to the full when in 1904 he produced at Leeds a setting of "Everyman," which is a landmark in the history of English Music. The success of this work was immediate and assured. Within a few years it was repeated at the festivals of Worcester, Sheffield, and Norwich, and at concerts of the London Choral Society and the Bach Choir. It pointed the way to a series of cantatas and other choral compositions in all of which, and notably in the Song of St. Francis, there breathes a like spirit of mysticism and a like fervour of religious emotion. Meanwhile the completeness of his equipment and the simplicity and geniality of his character gave him a special power of dealing with large popular audiences: his lectures both in London and in the provinces were crowded to overflowing; he was in great and continuous demand as a judge at musical competitions; it was by natural selection that at the outbreak of War he was appointed a musical organizer to the British forces. After demobilisation further honours awaited him: the Directorship of Welsh Music in 1919, a knighthood in 1922, the Gresham professorship in 1924, and in 1927 the organistship of St. George's, Windsor, where half a century before he had sung as a choir boy. Few of our musicians have touched the art on so many sides or have wrought for it more varied and distinguished service.

His writings lie within a comparatively narrow range. He has never been attracted by opera, or by any form of pageantry: his instrumental works are most characteristic in the smaller forms. He is at his best in the congenial task of setting the great religious poets, especially the mystics with whom he has close affinity: he is of the company of Vaughan and Crashaw and Traherne, and like them has penetrated to the inner shrine. Even in his lighter vein there is commonly a seriousness of purpose; only when he is writing for children and young people does he relax into playtime. But to all who love purity of style, beauty of sound, and intensity of devotion he is and will remain one of our national leaders, and the requital of his gift is in the lasting gratitude of his fellow-countrymen.

A tributary which for most of its course has run

through alien regions is the music of Frederick Delius. He was born in 1863 at Bradford, of naturalized German parents, and educated at first for a business career, the most incongruous choice that could have been devised for him. At the age of nineteen he was sent to an orange plantation in Florida, where, though he found the duties equally uncongenial, he employed his leisure time in the assiduous study of scores and musical treatises. The strain was brought to breaking-point by his father's refusal to let him follow his natural bent: in 1885 he shook himself clear of home influences and made his way to Germany and the Leipzig Conservatorium. Since 1890 he has lived chiefly in France; a remote and solitary figure brooding over his art in seclusion and equally indifferent to applause and criticism.

His first publication was a Légende for violin and orchestra (1892): his period of discipleship may be said to end with the symphonic poem "Paris," which appeared seven years later. From 1901, when he completed "A Village Romeo and Juliet," there has followed a succession of great and mature works: "Appalachia" and "Brigg Fair," "Sea Drift" and "A Song of the High Hills," "The Mass of Life," and "The Songs of Sunset," with their retinue of delightful idylls and elegies and their fellow adventurers in the forms of sonata and concerto. His music is intensely personal and introspective, a little lacking, it may be, in firmness of outline and definiteness of plan, most beautiful when it weaves, in a dreamland of its own, its texture and interplay of emotional colour. Many of its most pictorial pages are suggested by English scenes and English landscapes: an affinity which is the more significant because it was probably unconscious. Yet his distinctive qualities are not those of our national art; they adorn it as an exotic which we have learned to admire but which we can hardly claim.

A far more central and representative figure is Vaughan Williams, the most characteristically English among the composers of the present generation. Born in the Cotswolds and educated at the Royal College under Wood, Stanford, and Parry, he was brought up in the inner court of our native traditions: in 1905 he became an active member of the Folk Song Society, then recently inaugurated by Fuller Maitland, Miss Broadwood, and Cecil Sharp, and took a leading part in the collection and dissemination of its melodies. In 1907 the three Norfolk Rhapsodies brought his name into prominence: later in the same year he put the seal to his reputation by producing, at a Leeds festival, his choral setting of Whitman's Ode "Towards the Unknown Region." Its abundant promise was fulfilled when three years later he wrote the Sea Symphony for Leeds and the Tallis variations for Gloucester: then followed in succession the five mystical songs at Worcester, the Fantasia on Christmas Carols at Hereford, and the London Symphony which gathers, interprets, and enhances the humours and adventures of a great city. Its expression of robust and vigorous comedy, through sheer beauty of theme and richness of orchestral colour, finds a worthy pendant in the opera "Hugh the Drover" which, though not produced until ten years later, was completed about the same time. During

the War he served with the forces both in Salonika
and in France, and that experience, from which no
man returned unaltered, bore fruit both in the matur-
ing of his genius and in the deepening and widening
of its range. The Pastoral Symphony which he
wrote soon after his return is the very embodiment
of emotion recollected in tranquillity: the more
exquisitely serene and meditative because it has
known the beating of the storm. A like intensity
of controlled emotion animates his other works of
this period: the "Shepherds of the Delectable
Mountains," the Mass in G minor, the suite "Flos
Campi"[1] for viol, voices and orchestra, and the
oratorio "Sancta Civitas," which speaks from the
midst of the apocalyptic vision. And as these represent the graver and more serious aspects of his art,
so we may find a similar though divergent direction
of sympathy in his holiday mood, in the "Concerto
Accademico" which is no more austere than the
academic overture of Brahms, in the Cambridge
ballet on a nursery theme, and, above all, in the
brilliant Shakespearean comedy which is, at present
writing, his latest composition for the stage.

He possesses in a high degree the gift of handling
great choral masses and piling them layer by layer
into a firm architectonic scheme. The stones are
none the worse for being sometimes rough-hewn:
they are shaped by a hand which has won freedom
through mastery and set in their places with unerring judgment. As a melodist he is high in the
front rank: witness the cycle "On Wenlock Edge"
and the five mystical songs, and the settings of

[1] See Illustration O.

Stevenson and Rossetti; their limpid and trans-
lucent beauty flows in a clear stream from our native
hills. The present age has been largely preoccupied
with problems of technical skill, a "period of eager
experiment" in which the poet has sometimes been
subordinated to the craftsman. Vaughan Williams
has all the craftsmanship and all the spirit of adventure in its use, but to him as to every supreme artist
the poet comes first.

In his early days at the Royal College he formed
a close and abiding friendship with Gustav Holst
(*b.* 1874) on whose musical life he has exercised a
considerable influence. The two careers offer many
points of resemblance. Holst was also a west
countryman and a pupil of Stanford, a keen student
of folk song and of rural England: as Vaughan
Williams made his début with the Fen country and
the Norfolk Rhapsodies, so among Holst's earliest
compositions are the Somerset Rhapsody and the
Symphony on the Cotswolds. Both have an innate
tendency to mysticism, both have mastered and
touched to fine issues the free and flexible idiom of
the present time. In his early manhood Holst was
much attracted by the poetry and philosophy of
India, and between 1906 and 1911 composed an opera
"Savitri" and a series of choral hymns on subjects
from the Rigveda, the Mahabharata, and the poems
of Kalidasa. The texts of these were written in free
rhythmic prose and so adapted to the asymmetric
measures of five and seven which the composer has
so frequently employed in his later music. In melody
and treatment they show none of that "Orientalism"
which a priori critics attempted to find in them;

they are the outpourings of a soul trained under
Western skies and bringing to his Eastern studies
a philosophy of life with which he was already
in communion.

Despite weak health and a frail constitution he
served in the War as director of music to the British
forces in Salonika, and on his return added to his
many teaching posts a professorship at the Royal
College. But the impulse to composition was too
strong to be resisted, and even in these dark days he
heralded the dawn with two of his greatest masterpieces: the "Hymn of Jesus" for double-chorus, and
a superb cycle of orchestral tone - poems entitled
"The Planets." With these he came to his own: the
long period of waiting and preparation was accomplished, and the public acknowledgment of his
genius acclaimed the full maturity and fruition of its
power. His more recent works include two operas
—"The Perfect Fool" and "At the Boar's Head"—
a fugal overture and a fugal concerto, a setting of
Whitman's "Hymn to Death," a choral symphony,
the words of which are selected from Keats, an
Aubade for May morning, and a number of smaller
compositions in various forms. Like Vaughan
Williams he is still in full middle life and may yet
add fresh triumphs to the past. Enough has already
been won to show us that in him we have an artist
of great force and originality, uncompromising in
style, convincing in eloquence; a pioneer who has
opened to us new paths and has carried us with him
in their exploration.

The later representatives of our new music are
too diverse in aim to be gathered into a single

category, and in enumerating their chief names we can but follow an order which is roughly chronological. From the 'seventies come Rutland Boughton, who in 1914 founded the Glastonbury Festivals and inaugurated them with his masterpiece "The Immortal Hour"; Holbrooke, a versatile but unequal composer whose talent has been hindered by its own abundance; Cyril Scott, who has listened too readily to the twin sirens of atonality and metaphysics; John Ireland, whose close-wrought and scholarly art has too seldom allowed itself to speak out. From the 'eighties come Bax and Lord Berners, Bliss and Howells and Goosens, who have given us the "Garden of Fand," the "Fantasie Espagnole," the Colour Symphony, the "Sine nomine" fantasia, the "Eternal Rhythm," and many other important works, ranging from delicate imagination to sardonic humour and extending in their range the whole gamut of a rapidly developing technique. Youngest of the generation is Walton, who was born in the year 1902 and whose "Façade" and "Portsmouth Point" have already given him an assured position in the ranks of European music.

It remains to consider briefly some of the influences by which, during recent years, our English art has been fostered and encouraged. Chief among these is the munificence of the Carnegie Trust which, like the householder in the parable, has brought forth out of its treasure things new and old. From the establishment of the Trust in 1914 it has been a most generous friend to music, giving grants to concert societies and competition festivals and other similar institutions, especially to those whose work has spread to the poorer and more remote parts of the country. In 1917 it began a scheme for publishing compositions of high merit which the more commercial houses were too cautious or too conservative to undertake. During the ten years of its operation the scheme was triumphantly successful: at each annual meeting some three or four works were chosen for award, and among them were "The Travelling Companions" by Stanford, the "Immortal Hour" by Boughton, Holst's "Hymn to Jesus," the Hebridean Symphony by Bantock, the London Symphony by Vaughan Williams, a quartet and a quintet by Howells, and an orchestral rhapsody by Bliss. A still greater achievement is its monumental edition of Tudor Church music, the opening volume of which appeared in 1923 and which has revealed for the first time the treasures of our ecclesiastical compositions from Taverner to Gibbons. For three centuries the vast majority of these had been completely forgotten: the scores unedited, the parts lost or neglected in the dusty and remote shelves of libraries and choir cupboards: now through the labours of a few devoted scholars[1] and the far-sighted enterprise of the Carnegie Trustees we have come into possession of an inheritance which, it may be said advisedly, is comparable to that left by the Elizabethan drama.

When the Carnegie scheme of awards was first

---

[1] The work was at first entrusted solely to Sir Richard Terry. As it grew in bulk it was extended to a committee of other experts: Professor Buck, Dr. E. H. Fellowes, the Rev. A. Ramsbotham, and Miss Sylvia Warner. Dr. Fellowes, besides his services to Tudor Church Music, has produced a definitive edition of the Elizabethan Madrigals.

mooted some critics protested because it contained no provision for public performances: a complaint doubly unreasonable since it existed for another purpose which it amply fulfilled and since provision was already made in the Patrons' Fund Concerts at the Royal College. These were founded in 1903 on a generous benefaction from Sir Ernest Palmer, and have afforded to our younger artists, both creative and executive, a growing opportunity of recognition. These opportunities have been extended by local orchestras, notably that of Bournemouth, by the promenade concerts of Sir Henry Wood, and by other similar institutions. The British Music Society, constituted in 1918, has helped still further to enhance our prestige, and we may find a tribute to its work in the fact that it has been selected for headquarters by the International Society of Contemporary Music. Most powerful, both in the width of its range and in the concentration of its authority, is the musical department of the British Broadcasting Corporation, which affords to our composers their due share of opportunity and gives them the whole civilized world for audience. There is no doubt a danger that this concentration of authority may injuriously affect the practice and performance of music by separate orchestras and choral societies. If this danger be realised it will be a serious detriment to the progress of art in the country at large. England is a musical nation not only by listening, but by actively producing the music to which it listens, and to this practical and executive side every encouragement should be given. But the B.B.C. is strong enough to bear many brothers near the throne, and the width of its own area and influence may afford ample opportunities for co-operation.

This volume is chiefly a record of British musical composition: of its vicissitudes, its interruptions, and its gradual return towards the dignity and reputation which it once enjoyed. We should pass beyond our due bounds if we allotted a chapter, as we well might, to the executive artists, who even in our darkest period have been famous, and to the critics, scholars, and historians who have illustrated our course with so much learning and insight. Its principal characteristics, as known time after time in our annals, are strength, sanity, and tenderness: we are not by nature passionate, we have little taste for revolution; and hence while we avoid some foolish extravagances we miss also the great moments and crises of emotion which have sometimes glowed in the music of other lands. This is no disparagement: it is a very youthful criticism which is satisfied "à faire craquer les barrières," or thinks that vehemence is the only measure of power. We have our own vision of beauty: a vision of English skies and English woodlands, of Gainsborough and Constable, of Chaucer and Milton and Wordsworth. So far as our music can embody and express this ideal so far will it advance, firmly and confidently, along the lines of its great tradition as a living language.

ILLUSTRATIONS

" SUMER IS I-CUMEN IN "

" AGINCOURT "

" O ROSABELLA "

JOHN DUNSTABLE

O Rosabella, dolce amica mia
Non me lascia morire in cortesia.

"THE WESTERN WYNDE"

AS USED BY TAVERNER

SANCTUS FROM THE MASS, IN THREE PARTS

BYRD

M   177   E.M.

"ADIEU, SWEET AMARYLLIS"

WILBYE

"HENCE, CARE, THOU ART TOO CRUEL"

WEELKES

" THE SELF-BANISHED "

BLOW

" I ATTEMPT FROM LOVE'S SICKNESS TO FLY "

PURCELL

179

"O GO YOUR WAY," FROM THE JUBILATE IN D

PURCELL

I

DR. BULL'S AYRE AS TRANSCRIBED BY SMART

J

THE SAME WITH KEY SIGNATURE ADDED

(J)

180

"GOD SAVE THE KING" (EARLIEST DATED COPY 1745)

BARCAROLLE FROM CONCERTO IN F MINOR

STERNDALE BENNETT

"WASH ME THROUGHLY"

S. S. WESLEY

L

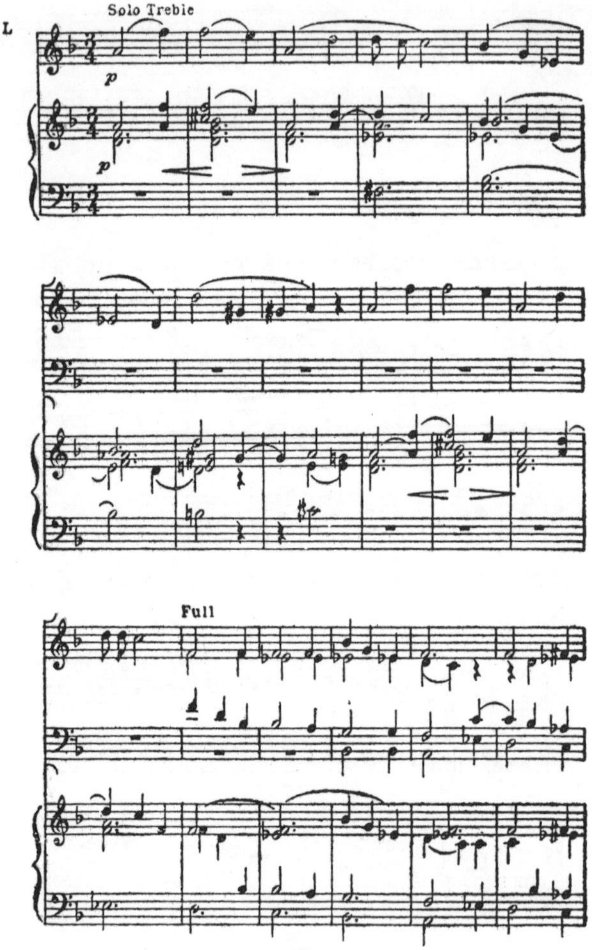

"WASH ME THROUGHLY"

"THERE IS AN OLD BELIEF"

PARRY

184

"THERE IS AN OLD BELIEF"

"THE KINGDOM"

ELGAR

186

"FLOS CAMPI"

VAUGHAN WILLIAMS

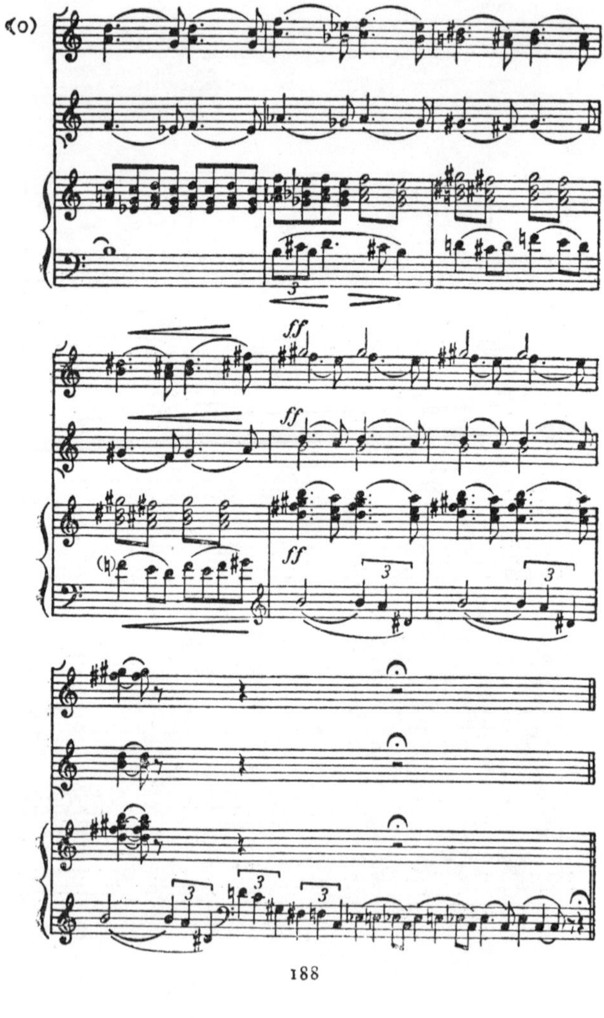
(O)
ff
ff
ff
3